Sonja Ulrike Klug

Passion for Compasses

Medieval Master Builders and their Cathedral Building Plans

Bibliografische Information der Deutschen Nationalbibliothek:

Die Deutsche Nationalbibliothek verzeichnet diese Publikation in der Deutschen Nationalbibliographie; detaillierte bibliografische Daten sind im Internet über http://dnb-d-nb.de abrufbar.

Menzenberger Str. 22, 53604 Bad Honnef, info@kluges-verlag.de (Germany)

1st edition 2024

ISBN: 978-3-910321-20-5 **(Paperback)**

ISBN: 978-3-910321-23-6 **(Hardcover)**

ISBN: 978-3-910321-21-2 **(E-Book)**

ISBN: 978-3-910321-22-9 **(Audiobook)**

Original edition in German:

Sonja Ulrike Klug: "Zauberer des Zirkels. Die Frage nach den Bauplänen des Mittelalters." Oppenheim: Nünnerich-Asmus Verlag & Media, 2020. (Germany).

Production of the printed books: Amazon Distribution

Press reviews of the original German edition of this book

Published under the title "Zauberer des Zirkels" (2020):

"'Zauberer des Zirkels' is more than a work on the history of art and architecture in the Middle Ages. Medieval architecture was an expression of medieval culture. Thus, Klug's presentation includes cultural, cognitive, linguistic, literary, mathematical, graphic and technical aspects that not only support her thesis, but also provide interesting approaches to considering other phenomena of medieval culture.

Despite the demanding content the book is written in an understandable and entertaining way. Klug argues convincingly, using numerous quotations and examples to make her train of thought clear. Important findings and conclusions are highlighted in the text, and illustrations provide additional clarity. ...

Its multidimensional and interdisciplinary approach makes the book an interesting study of medieval culture and goes beyond the consideration of purely architectural phenomena. Klug's thoroughly researched work is therefore not only recommended for readers interested in architectural and art history, but also offers valuable insights and food for thought into the history of the Middle Ages."

(https://blog.histofact.de, 2020/09/28)

"I really liked the combination of engaging and sometimes humorous writing style with meticulous documentation supported by credible sources. The author not only demonstrates intelligence but also thoroughness and empathy."

(Online reviewer *Gute_Buecher999*)

"Ms. Klug clears up the misconceptions of historians and other authors and brings together proven evidence in such a way that we gain a new perspective on the great buildings, churches and cathedrals of the period. ...

The author's arguments are factual and comprehensible – there are at most one or two conclusions that one would like to interject with a 'Yes, but ...', at least once. However, these are by no means the cornerstones for her argumentation. ...

One can appreciate not only Sonja Ulrike Klug's expertise, but also her pleasant writing style. She explains her theory in an easy-to-understand and well-founded manner while incorporating historical context, which refreshes and supplements the reader's knowledge.

'Zauberer des Zirkels' is therefore not only interesting for experts, but for any reader who is enthusiastic about medieval architecture and history!"

(https://www.nightshade-magazin.de, 2020/09/17)

Contents

1. Master builders and master plans in the Middle Ages – Introduction

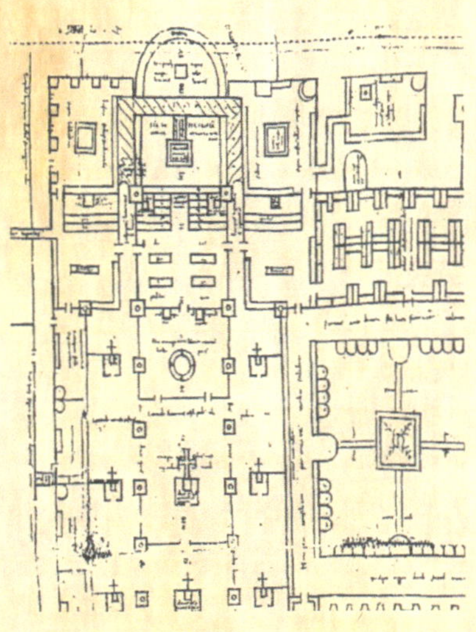

1.1 The "data" of the cathedrals

The fact that *Notre-Dame de Paris Cathedral* was massively damaged by fire in 2019 is – one might assume – not actually a bad thing. Although no medieval building plans have survived, scientific 3D data exist. These were created by various experts before the disaster and, along with further recordings, are being converted into a complete 3D model as part of a research project.[1]

3D data – three-dimensional and undoubtedly computer-generated survey data – will allow the cathedral to be faithfully reconstructed. Data that simulate, true to scale, what the building looked like in every facet and detail before the fire; data that allow almost every inch of the entire building to be shown from any direction and in a perfect 360-degree panoramic view; data that can be zoomed in on the smallest detail and out to lofty heights.

With such a complete design basis, rebuilding *Notre-Dame de Paris* must be easy, apart from the practicalities of construction. Since 2019, the fire at *Notre-Dame* has also made those responsible for other churches sit up and take notice: they have commissioned the digital surveying of architectural monuments to ensure faithful reconstruction in case future fires destroy larger parts of them.

In the Middle Ages, it was much more difficult to rebuild a church after it had burned down, which happened very often and was usually caused by lightning striking in a tower. How was a cathedral constructed (or reconstructed) in an era when there were no highly accurate computer-generated 3D data – indeed, when construction plans did not even exist?

A remarkable phenomenon of medieval architecture is the lack of building and construction plans, which are designed in such a way that they can be used to plan buildings as a whole. Partial plans of individual construction elements exist for a number of buildings, but overall plans have never been found.

Compared to the Romanesque period, the Gothic period saw great advances in building construction: the naves were wider than in the Romanesque period, the vault construction allowed for higher ceilings due to the use of pointed arches, and in addition, the towers reached unprecedented heights of more than 131 yd. In addition, there were other innovations such as artfully designed and large stained glass windows. Despite all these advances over earlier buildings or predecessor churches from the Romanesque period, no overall plans, sketches or construction drawings have yet been found until today – neither for the Romanesque nor for the Gothic period.

1.2 Built for eternity without plans?

Nevertheless, historians of architecture and art often assume that there must have been not only general plans, but also many other plans, which were used to construct the buildings in advance. For example, the structural engineer Dietrich Conrad, in his German standard work *Kirchenbau im Mittelalter* ("Church Construction in the Middle Ages"), states that about 2,200 copies of *medieval* plans have survived, but

> *"no drawings of the mass of medieval buildings have been preserved."* [2]

Have these construction plans ever existed? Have they been lost, burned, deliberately or accidentally destroyed? Are they, as the art historian Günther Binding notes,

> *"a mythical figure that is given reality and helped to actually exist? "*[3]

Or did they never exist?

Conrad notes a vacuum in the stock of drawings, especially between the 4th and the 13th centuries, which also surprises other architectural historians time and again. Merely one exception seems to have been existed: the famous monastery plan of St. Gall, an ideal plan that was created around 825 (vf. Figure 1), but it was never implemented 1:1 in terms of construction. It seems to have served as a kind of "creative planning basis".

From the point of view of modern architects, engineers and structural engineers, it is indeed hard to imagine that the master builders of the early and high Middle Ages would have erected complex churches, castles and other buildings *without* drawings. The historian Max Hasak agrees with Conrad that architectural drawings have always been *"necessary, even indispensable aids to construction planning"* at all times.[4] Konrad Hecht, author of a well-known work on the St. Gallen monastery plan, believes that in the Middle Ages a building

> *"was prepared not differently than today: with a design developed on the drawing board".* [5]

However, this is contradicted by the fact that detailed plans for individual elements of some buildings on wood or stone have survived from the time before the 13th century, but no draft or rough plans for *entire buildings* have survived.[6] It is only from the mid-13th century that plans at a scale of 1:1 as well as *"reasonably proportionate drawings"* [7] are preserved, as Binding notes. Scaled plans have existed since the 15th century.

The oldest true-to-scale plan dates from the 1420s from Bologna. A significant increase in the number of architectural drawings can be observed from the middle of the 14th century[8], and since the middle of the 15th century the number of architectural drawings has been on the rise.[9] From the 15th century onwards, drawings became legally binding and were part of the master craftsman's examination in some stonemasons' workshops (Bauhütten).[10]

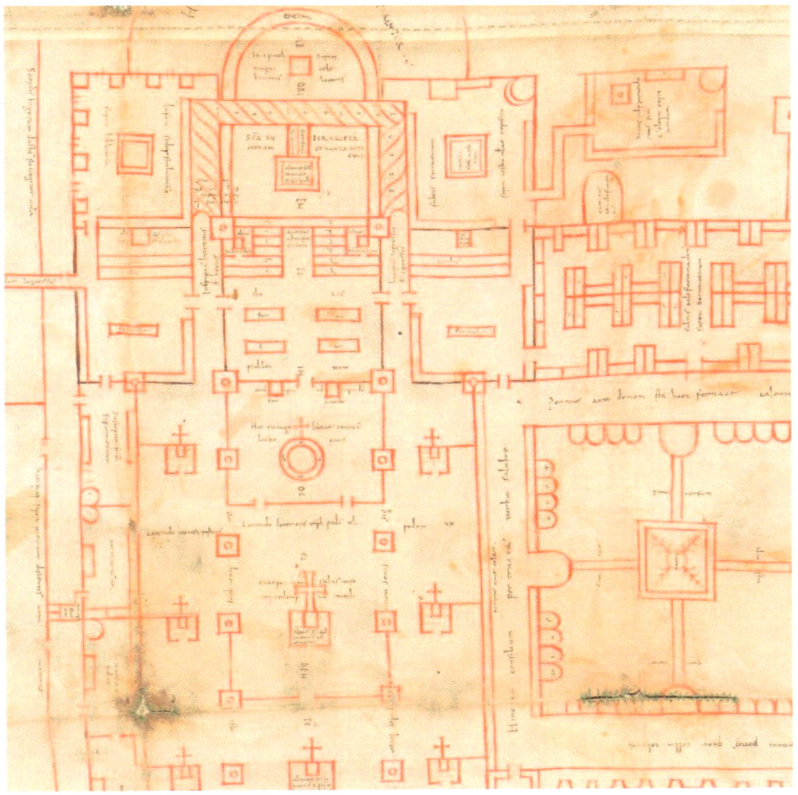

Figure 1: Small section of the plan of St. Gall monastery (on parchment). The lines were drawn freehand without compass or ruler, using marked pinpricks (cf. section 3.4).

1.3 Speculations about the whereabouts of the plans

The "gap" in the existence of building plans until the middle of the 14th century is explained by many architectural historians as having been lost or deliberately destroyed:

> *"Such drawings must once have numbered in the thousands. Only a vanishingly small part of them has survived. This remaining stock is almost entirely due to the preservation efforts of the stonemasons' workshops (Bauhütten) of western and southern Germany,"* says Hecht.[11]

Conrad agrees:

> *"The lack of drawings of buildings from Roman times to the 13th century can be explained by loss. Parchment and later paper – the main writing materials – were always particularly endangered by fire and water. [...] In these centuries, however, it was believed that what was built in stone would last forever and from this it was concluded that there was no need to preserve a drawing after the completion of a building. Due to the value of the drawing material (parchment and paper were very expensive), direct destruction was out of the question. The drawings were erased or scraped off and the newly obtained writing material (palimpsest) or the free 'backs' were used."* [12]

Jean Gimpel, an internationally renowned specialist in the history of medieval technology and author of the well-known book "The Cathedral Builders" among others, agrees with Conrad that there would have been no reason to keep construction plans of completed buildings, and therefore they would have been destroyed.[13]

The engineer Paul Booz, former master builder of the cathedral in Freiburg im Breisgau (Germany), believes that drawings must have existed before the 13th century, but that they were destroyed during the transition from Romanesque to Gothic architecture because they were no longer usable.[14] However, the division into distinct stylistic periods, such as Romanesque and Gothic, came much later. At the beginning of the Gothic period no one could foresee the further development of building styles or techniques. From the point of view of the former master builders, the transition from Romanesque to Gothic period was smooth. What we now consider a "different style" was certainly seen rather a "progress" in the art of building, as the Gothic period allowed for taller and wider church buildings with larger window areas.

Figure 2: Schematic representation of a section of the stained glass window *Histoire des Saint Silvestre,* created around 1220, in the southeast ambulatory of Chartres Cathedral, with stonemasonry tools (hammer, pick, square, mortar trowel, stencils) and building elements (column, cornice and capital). A construction plan is not visible.

All in all, as we can see, there is a wealth of different opinions and interpretations as to why so few construction plans were preserved until the 13th century. The "flourishing" speculations suggest that unidentified causes underlie the phenomenon.

Finally, Conrad comes to a conclusion that is shared by other authors:

> *"The state of building since the 4th century, despite all discontinuities, makes it quite simply inconceivable that the buildings could have been erected without preparatory work in the form*

> *of drawings. Thus, it should be noted once again that the absence of medieval architectural drawings before the 13th century does not permit the conclusion that there were no drawings in that period."* [15]

I will show below that Conrad, Hasak, Hecht, Gimpel, Booz and other historians of architecture and art are nevertheless wrong when they assume a continuum of construction knowledge since antiquity or since Vitruvius and when they think that most plans must have been lost or deliberately destroyed.

Medieval design plans from the time before the 13th century did not disappear, but do not exist at all – despite the skill of the master builders of that time and the outstanding architectural achievements that can still be seen today in the Romanesque and Gothic churches, and in some cases also in the castles.

Beyond the history of art and the plans themselves, I will show this by tracing the cultural-historical lines of the epoch from the 11th to the 16th century, thus illuminating the subject from different perspectives:

- The availability of writing materials in the Middle Ages (papyrus, parchment, paper) and the nature of their use or applicability gives a first indication of why the number of surviving plans is comparatively small.
- Researchers have compiled a large number of sources on the level of literacy of the European population between the 4th and 17th centuries. They provide a reliable and sometimes surprising picture, which includes the profession of architect.
- The typical characteristics of oral or preliterate cultures compared to literate ones, where script and writing were common, shed light

on the way people in the Middle Ages perceived and dealt with the written form.

- A linguistic analysis of some key formulations in Villard de Honnecourt's sketchbook in comparison to works by other authors provides further insight into the self-image of (book) authors of the Middle Ages and their relationship to the audience.
- The way in which some of the surviving plans are used allows conclusions to be drawn about supposedly missing plans.
- A comparative cultural analysis of Islamic architecture of the same period reveals that the Arab world is also familiar with the problem of "lost" drawings for epochal buildings, especially important mosques and medreses, from the 8th to the 14th century.
- The discovery of a mistranslation of Vitruvius shows the origin of the statement that in the Middle Ages building had to be done with the help of plans.
- Medieval education, including architectural training prior to the Renaissance, demonstrates the influence of building plans on the development of the architectural profession.
- The mathematical know-how available in the Middle Ages makes clear what master builders may or may not have known.
- The study of construction and construction instruments, especially different types of compasses, shows the possibilities and limitations of medieval planning and drawing.
- Closely related to the instruments is the art of drawing, which developed progressively from the 15th century onwards, producing various types of projection of three-dimensional bodies onto a two-dimensional surface and thus revolutionizing technical drawing.

2. Papyrus, parchment, and paper – the long road to writing media and written language

2.1 Mobile, easily portable and affordable writing materials

When Papyrus perished

In today's world, we have plenty of writing materials at our disposal, especially paper. For every note, every draft, every type of writing, every drawing, there is always enough inexpensive paper in all imaginable formats, colors, and qualities. The fact that this was not the case in earlier centuries, and that there was a real shortage of paper as well as other writing materials, is hard to understand from today's perspective. But the "luxury" of always having enough inexpensive paper available has only existed in Europe since the late 19th century.

Not much is known about the writing materials of the Middle Ages, except that parchment was predominantly used. Unfortunately, there are still a number of errors circulating in the specialist literature, mainly concerning the times when papyrus, parchment and paper were used and the reasons for their use. Here is a small compilation of inaccurate statements:

- The historian Otto Mazal believes that paper replaced papyrus as a writing material because papyrus production ceased under the pressure of growing paper production.[16] But this is not true: There is a gap of about 500 years between the cessation of papyrus production and the spread of paper in Europe, during which time paper was unknown and only parchment was used.
- Jean Gimpel claims that plans on parchment began to appear more frequently in the 14th and 15th centuries because *"the price of parchment had fallen in the meantime."* [17] But the opposite was true. From

the 14th century onwards, paper became more and more widespread, and it became popular in the 15th century precisely because its price dropped extremely compared to parchment. Parchment, on the other hand, remained expensive and scarce. Construction plans, as well as other written documents, were increasingly drawn on paper instead of parchment from the 15th century onward.[18]

- The paleographer Karin Schneider believes that papyrus was replaced by parchment in the Middle Ages because the latter proved to be much more durable.[19] This is true in some respects, but parchment was already known as a writing material since pre-Christian times, and not just in Europe. This raises the question of why papyrus was used in Europe for so long, if parchment was supposedly more advantageous.
- The Germanist Karl-Heinz Göttert thinks that paper is an invention of the Arabs[20], although they only acted as intermediaries or merchants between East and West. Paper is a Chinese invention.

The reason for the demise of papyrus and parchment as writing materials, and the time when paper was introduced and spread throughout Europe are largely unknown in terms of cultural history. However, the development and availability of mobile, easily portable, and sufficiently inexpensive writing materials is important in terms of when construction drawings might have been created.

In Europe, from about the 5th century B. C.[21] to about the 7th century A. D., people wrote on papyrus, made from the papyrus plant, traditionally and apparently exclusively in Egypt, where it had been known since the 4th or 3rd millennium B. C.[22] For centuries, it was exported from there in large quantities to Europe via Byblos, a city in Syria, and exchanged for other goods. Papyrus was also the predominant writing material of ancient Greece and the Roman period. Before that, only clay, stone, wood, or leather had been available, but papyrus offered many advantages: It is pliable, transportable, easy to write on, and can be glued into rolls of any length. It was papyrus, with its massive distribution, that spurred the development of ancient scholarship and writing in antiquity.

Due to the many political crises and upheavals in Egypt, which was conquered several times by different Islamic groups from the 7th century onwards, there was apparently a crisis in papyrus production. Some researchers believe that the papyrus areas shrank massively due to the expansion of agriculture[23], causing the papyrus plants to wither. Since the 7th or 8th century, no more writing material could be produced from the plant or exported.

The last written documents in Christian Europe on papyrus date from about the middle of the 7th century from the Merovingian dynasty. The very last verifiable papyrus document was issued by the Vatican in 1057, but by that time the Vatican was using parchment almost exclusively and was probably using up its last supplies of papyrus.[24] Without papyrus, Europe "sat on dry land", and the previously flourishing distribution and reproduction of written documents dried up. Only in Italy the situation was somewhat better, as papyrus continued to grow in large quantities in Sicily where the plant was probably used to make writing materials until the 12th or 13th century.[25] It is possible that Sicily already had access to paper exports from the Arab world.

Parchment replaces papyrus

After the loss of papyrus, people in Europe turned to parchment, which was already common and occasionally used in in both Europe and the Orient in ancient times.[26] Parchment is made from the skins of cattle, calves, sheep, and goats, although sheepskin was the preferred material in Europe. Unlike leather, parchment is not tanned. The skins of the animals are soaked, cleaned and placed in a lime solution to remove hair and any adhering particles of flesh. The skin is then stretched in a frame and treated with knives to remove hair and imperfections and to create a smooth surface. After drying, the parchment is smoothed with chalk and pumice stone to make it writable, and cut to the desired size (cf. Figure 3).[27]

Parchment has the advantage of being more durable than papyrus, it can be written on both sides and lasts longer. Both papyrus and parchment can be washed and reused. This is evidenced by the numerous so-called palimpsests – parchment sheets (and very few preserved papyri) whose texts were erased so that they could be reused and re-inscribed.

But parchment also has its disadvantages: As an organic material, it is sensitive to moisture. If it comes into direct contact with water, it will begin to rot after a while. However, undesirable changes can also occur without direct contact with water and can be caused by excessively humid air. This allows the parchment to turn glassy and to expand; when it dries, it shrinks and becomes wavy. If the parchment is repeatedly moistened and dries again, the ink on it will flake off.

Figure 3: "The Parchment Maker" or "Permennter" From the *Ständebuch* by Jost Amman / Hans Sachs (Nuremberg 1568) – plus the text by Hans Sachs:

"I buy skins of sheep, rams and goats. I put the skins in the pickle. Then I clean them and stretch each single skin on a frame. After that I scrape it and make parchment out of it, with a lot of work in my house. From ears and claws I make glue, and sell it all at home."

Original in German:
„Ich kauff Schaffell / Böck / vnd die Geiß /
Die Fell leg ich denn in die beyß /
Darnach firm ich sie sauber rein /
Spann auff die Ram jeds Fell allein/
Schabs darnach / mach Permennt darauß /
Mit grosser arbeit in mein Hauß /
Auß ohrn vnd klauwen seud ich Leim /
Das alles verkauff ich daheim.“)

Obviously, all of this has negative consequences for architectural drawings. They could become distorted in their proportions or illegible. This is pointed out by parchment experts as well as by architectural historians who have studied medieval drawings on parchment.[28]

Another disadvantage of parchment was its high price. Because it was so expensive, it was mainly used for documents and books, but was not usually available for everyday writing. In this case, wax tablets were used as mnemonic devices (cf. section 3.3) – or one simply had to give up writing.

From about the 12th century, the volume of written correspondence in Europe increased considerably, especially in political administration and at courts. This is clearly illustrated by the example of England: between 1250 and 1350, the amount of writing materials and sealing wax increased tenfold to twentyfold. At the beginning of the 13th century only a few dozen sheep had to give their lives on the occasion of a royal court day, but by 1283 the number of animals had risen to 500.[29] The situation was similar in France, the Vatican, and Germany. Statistical counts showed that the number of documents increased tenfold from the 11th to the 12th century and doubled again in the 13th century; at the same time, the number of court chanceries increase significantly.[30] According to a statistical study, manuscript production increased ninefold throughout Western Europe from the 11th to the 12th century, and quadrupled again from the 12th to the 13th century.[31] In the absence of other writing materials, parchment was used without exception.

As the number of written documents increased, it was foreseeable that parchment would become increasingly difficult to supply. Animal skins were too expensive in the long run, especially since animals served multiple functions as food and raw material suppliers for the textile industry. It was not possible to slaughter animals for every document, every letter, every court decision (or every architectural drawing) that needed to be written. This would have led to the complete exodus of cattle, calves, sheep and goats, whose wool and milk were urgently needed for clothing and food.

Concerning wool, for example, there were long-term contracts between agricultural suppliers, e. g. the Cistercian Order in England, and the clothing industry in Italy.

If papyrus had still been available at that time, it would have been obvious that it would have continued to be used as a writing material in addition to parchment due to the high demand. But the paleographic evidence clearly shows that this was not the case: papyrus had already completely disappeared in Europe by the 11th century.

The need for writing materials grew due to the lack of papyrus. Parchment was expensive and not in short supply. This was the situation when the Gothic period began to flourish in Europe in the 12th century, and Europeans first came into contact with the new, unknown type of paper through Muslim-occupied Spain.

The Umayyads, who had been driven out of their ancestral empire by the Abassids, wandered through North Africa and finally founded the Emirate of Cordoba in the south of the Iberian Peninsula in al-Andalus in 756 A. D. They brought with them the already well-developed Arabic knowledge and literature and, within one or two centuries, also introduced the know-how of paper production, which the Arabs had taken over from the Chinese. Around 750, the Arab world first came into contact with paper invented by the Chinese through the trading hub of Samarkand (now Uzbekistan), located on the Silk Road, and the region around Khorasan.

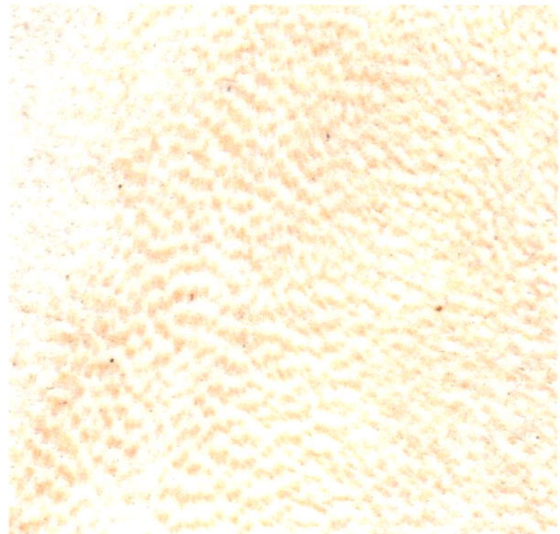

Figure 4: Structural comparison of papyrus (left) and parchment (right). Papyrus consists of transverse and longitudinal fibers of the plant held together by starch. The parchment reveals the uneven surface of animal skin.

The invention of paper in China and its spread across the Arab world

In China, an extensive bureaucratic state system had already developed since the 11th century B. C. Initially, bones, shells, ivory, turtle shells, stone, clay, and later bamboo strips and silk had been used as writing materials. In the course of time, bamboo increasingly gained the upper hand, but its enormous weight and its format, which was limited to narrow strips and thus short texts, proved to be a great weakness. Once, when the imperial book collection had to be transported, 2,000 cartloads were needed. In addition, the bulky bamboo texts in the library were difficult to arrange in a clear order. So Cai Lun (ca. 50 – 121 A. D.) – a Chinese official and advisor to the emperor, responsible among other things for furnishing the imperial household and making furniture and swords – was commissioned to develop a better writing material.[32]

Cai Lun is said to have invented paper in China around 105 A. D., but he probably improved already existing manufacturing processes. Fragments of Chinese paper made before this time have been found. The invention of papermaking was an ongoing process rather than a single event.[33]

Cai Lun is said to have originated the following papermaking process: The bark of the mulberry tree is soaked in water and intensively decomposed. It is pounded with a large mortar to break down the fibers and allow them to swell until they form a kind of pulp. A scooping sieve is used to manually scoop out each sheet of paper from the pulp. The sheet forms a kind of fiber mat in the sieve. After the liquid has been squeezed out, the paper is hung to dry until it is ready to be written on. It is often smoothed with a stone before.

Instead of the bark of the mulberry tree, which does not grow everywhere, other raw materials were used in the same way in China and in the Arab world, depending on the region, e. g. hemp, fishing nets, flax, linen and, above all, rags from old, worn-out textiles.[34] Rags served the Arabs, and later the Europeans as raw material for paper production.

The production of paper from mulberry bark is not entirely dissimilar to that of papyrus. The crucial difference, however, is the more intensive decomposition (maceration) of the raw materials, which allows to obtain the maximum of paper sheets from the pulp of the raw material. In papyrus production, the plant fibers are not softened, but cut into strips. Two sheets at a time are laid horizontally and vertically on top of each other and beaten until they are bonded together by the release of starch, which acts like glue. After drying and polishing, the papyrus is ready to be written on.

According to Cai Lun's manufacturing process, paper spread all over the world within about 1,500 years. It came to the East in the Asian region, especially to Korea and Japan, via missionary Buddhist monks. From China, it reached Europe in the West via the Silk Road with the help of the Arabs, who saw themselves as traders and merchants in the tradition of Mohammed. The Arabs first learned about paper around 750 in Samarkand, on the border with China, but did not use it at first. But when the decline of papyrus became painfully apparent in the Muslim world as well, and when it became clear that the demand for writing materials could not be met by parchment alone, the Arabs began to set up their own paper manufactories and run them according to the Chinese model. This happened at the end of the 8th or at the beginning of the 9th century.[35]

The first paper manufactory was established in the largest Islamic center, the capital Baghdad, soon followed by other manufactories in Cairo, Damascus and further important Islamic cities. From then on, paper was used as a consumer good and was also exported to the Middle East via the Silk Road. It reached the European region via the Mediterranean Sea, although it is still not entirely clear whether it first arrived in Sicily or Spain.

When paper finally became available in sufficient quantities as a writing material, a veritable cultural flowering began in the Muslim world: Science, literature, and education began to develop in leaps and bounds. While Europe was in a deep intellectual slumber, the Arab culture was soon several centuries ahead. In 825, under the Abbasid Caliph al-Mamum, the famous "House of Wisdom" was founded in Baghdad, a scientific academy where numerous works from ancient Greece were translated into Arabic. Mathematics, astronomy, medicine and literature flourished, and political rulers as well as wealthy private citizens of the Arab world maintained and cultivated extensive libraries. In the 11th century, Baghdad boasted more than a hundred bookstores.[36]

In Arab-occupied Spain, as before in Baghdad, a cultural flowering developed with universities and scholars, many of whom found their way to Spain from Baghdad. In cities such as Cordoba, Xativa (near Valencia), Seville and Toledo, paper manufactories had been established in the 11th century.[37] While even the Vatican library contained barely 2,000 volumes until the 14th century, the library of Al-Hakam II in Cordoba is said to have contained 400,000 volumes in the 10th century, with the index of works alone comprising 44 volumes.[38]

As is well known, the Spanish kings, in the so-called Reconquista, reconquered and rechristianized the Islamic-occupied Spain in several stages over several centuries. As early as 1086, Toledo, located roughly in the geographic center of Spain, was recaptured. Toledo was a city where Muslims, Jews, and Christians lived together peacefully for centuries, even after the Reconquista.

The writing material of the "unbelievers" reaches Christian Europe

In Toledo, Christians seem to have come into contact for the first time not only with the Arab culture, but also with paper as a writing material. This was caused by Petrus Venerabilis (1092 – 1156), abbot of the monastery of Cluny from 1122 to 1150. He visited Cordoba and Toledo and commissioned the first translation of the Quran and other Islamic scriptures into Latin at the famous translators' school in Toledo.

The Toledo School of Translators played a special role as a "relay station" between the Arab culture and the European culture. It initiated the further development of European culture, which began to catch up intellectually from the 12th century. Thanks to the school of translators many lost Greek and Latin manuscripts of antiquity, gathered in laborious searches over thousands of miles, were translated from ancient Greek into Arabic for the Muslims and then, on behalf of Europeans, first from Arabic in turn into Latin, the scholarly language of the Middle Ages. The world-famous School of Translators in Toledo was headed by Archbishop Gerhard of Cremona (c. 1114 – 87), who translated, among others, the works of Hippocrates, Archimedes, Galen, Ptolemy's *Almagest* and Euclid's *Elements* from Arabic into Latin.

When Petrus Venerabilis held a Quran in his hands for the first time, he also came into contact with paper for the first time. What he thought about the Quran and the new writing material paper is recorded in his "Treatise against the Jews" (in Latin: *Tractatus contra iudaeos)* and it is unfortunately not very flattering:

> *"God in heaven, says the Jew, reads the Talmud. But what kind of book is this [= the Quran]? It looks like what we use for reading every day, made of sheepskin, goatskin or calfskin [= parchment] or of (bulrush) bark from the swamplands of the Orient [= papyrus], but it is made of the scraps of old clothes [= rags], from which a piece of cloth of worthless texture [= paper] is made. It is inscribed with bird feathers or sharpened reed feathers and colored ink."*[39]
>
> (Original in Latin: *"Legit, inquit (iudaeus), Deus in Coelis librum Talmuth. Sed cuiusmodi librum? Si talem quales quotidie in usu legendi habemus utique ex pellibus arietum, hircorum, vel vitulorum, sive ex biblis, vel juncis orientalium paludum aut ex rasuris veterum pannorum, sive ex qualibet alia viliore materia compactos, et pennis avium vel calamis palastrium locorum, qualibet tinctura infectis descriptos".)*[40]

Apparently, Petrus does not think much of paper; he considers it an inferior material. Subliminally, he associates the inferior material quality with the content of the Quran. Paper was the "writing material of the unbelievers", which they used for their religious writings; accordingly, he was skeptical.

Despite these prejudices, Petrus' book project, the *Collectio Toletana* ("Collection of Toledo"), had a pioneering character for European cultural history as well as for Christian Europe's acquaintance with paper in the first half of the 12th century. However, it would take another century and a half for paper to establish itself as a writing material in Europe.

With the Christian conquest of the Iberian Peninsula and the retreat of the Arabs, the manufacture of paper passed more and more into the hands of Jews and Christians after 1238.[41] However, it was not the Spaniards but the Italians who spread it throughout Europe, starting with the enterprising Genoese, who had already been trading with Muslim and then with Christian Spain for several centuries, shipping their goods across the Mediterranean Sea. It was in Genoa, probably between 1210 and 1232, that the first paper manufactory on Italian soil was established, as the growing demand made it cheaper to produce paper locally than to import it from Spain. Bologna, Venice, Padua, Lucca, Amalfi and other important trading cities[42] soon followed with their own paper manufactories.

The oldest surviving European paper document is a bilingual Greek-Arabic edict written in 1109 by Countess Adelaide del Vasto, regent of Sicily and Queen of Jerusalem.[43] Also among the oldest paper documents in Europe are the extensive files of the Genoese notary Giovanni Scriba, dating from 1154 to 1164.[44] The oldest surviving German paper manuscript dates from 1246 and is the register book of the Passau cathedral deacon Albert Behaim, created in Lyon.[45]

The breakthrough of mass production and distribution of paper in Europe

Italy had a particularly great need for writing materials due to its extensive notarial system. Perhaps for this reason, the breakthrough in papermaking occurred around 1276 in the Italian town of Fabriano in the Marc Ancona. This finally led to its spread throughout Central Europe. The Italians improved on the Sino-Arabic production process by making the first use of mill technology (cf. Figure 5), which had been introduced in Europe in the 11th century and made the work easier. Water mills were used, for example, to grind grain, but also to grind fabrics.[46]

Water-powered pounding hammers were used to crush the raw materials, so that labor, previously done by hand, pounder and mortar with the help of many workers, was carried out more effectively and more quickly "by machine" or "automatically". This made it possible to process larger quantities of raw materials into a pulp (the raw material) in a shorter time. Even though each sheet of paper still had to be individually scooped out of the pulp by hand using a scooping sieve, the time savings and the larger production volumes were considerable compared to the Chinese-Arabian manufacturing process.

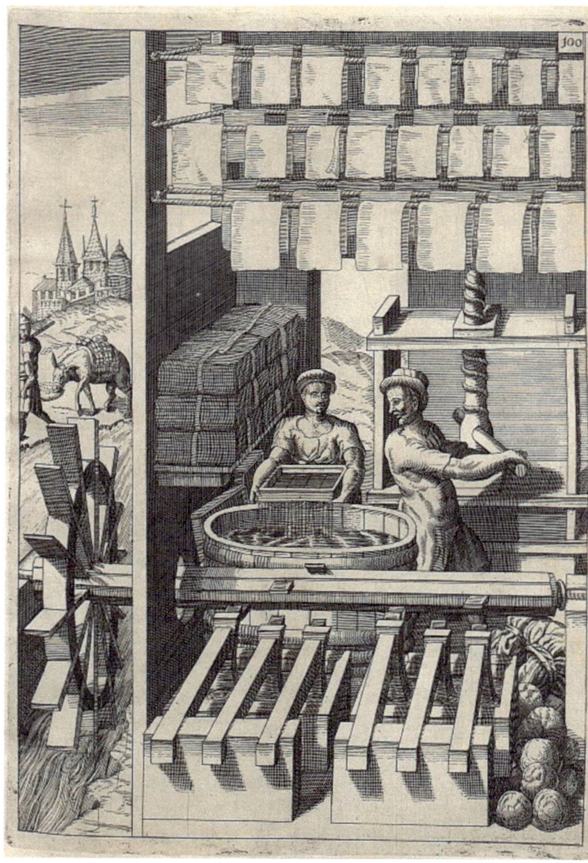

Figure 5: European paper mill (copperplate engraving by Jacobo Stradanus from his work "Artificial short treatise of various wind, water, horse and hand mills" (in German: *Kunstliche Abriß allerhand Wasser Wind Roß und Handt Mühlen*, Frankfurt/Main, ca. 1618).

To the left of the house, a paddle wheel driven by a water gradient moves the horizontal camshaft that enters the house. The camshaft drives the pounding hammers for two vats in which the rags and used textiles are crushed. They are shown on the right in their raw state as bales falling out of sacks; this is how they are delivered by rag pickers. Behind the camshaft is the circular vat containing the pulp, from which the papermaker is just scooping a sheet of paper with the scooping sieve. Next to him, a journeyman uses a large press to squeeze the water out of the freshly scooped paper, placing felts between the sheets. Afterwards, in the attic, the half-dried leaves are hung on strings to dry completely. In the background on the left, the sheets of paper are tied into bales, ready for sale. – The work processes, shown here compressed and shortened in terms of the work done in one room, usually took up an entire house, in which the papermaker's family lived and worked. Often 10 to 15 people were involved in papermaking. It can be seen that the papermaker's house is located on a watercourse outside the town, visible in the upper left, as was generally the case with mills.

The efficient use of water power to break down and process raw materials made the difference in finally making paper a mass product in Europe. In addition to several other technical improvements, the Italians also introduced the watermark, which was unkown in the Arab and Chinese worlds. Nowadays, watermark research makes it possible to trace the export routes and manufacturing sites of surviving papers back centuries.

Once the mass production of paper began, there was no stopping it. Growing quantities of paper were produced and exported from Italy to Spain, France, Germany and England, and later even to the Arab world. Water-powered paper mills were soon established in other European countries as well, for example in Troyes (France) in 1348 and in Nuremberg (Germany) in 1390. More paper mills followed, especially in important trading cities: Ravensburg in 1391 or 1393, Augsburg in 1407, Strasbourg in 1415, Lübeck in 1420, Basel (Switzerland) in 1440, Wartenfels in 1460, Kempten in 1468, St. Pöltgen (Austria) in 1469, Stevenage (England) in 1494. By the end of the 16th century, there were already 190 paper mills in Germany alone[47]; trading cities such as Ravensburg, Augsburg, and Nuremberg maintained seven to ten mills simultaneously.

From about 1370, paper was generally available in Germany, first still as an imported product from Italy or France, and later as a domestic product.[48] With paper, the increasing demand for a continuously available writing material could now be *gradually* met in Europe, and the age of parchment *slowly* came to an end. Paper did not immediately replace parchment. For about a century, it was common to use both parchment and paper for written documents and bound books. In the 14th century, 69 percent of book production is said to have been covered by parchment, in the 15th century only 30 percent.[49] By about 1450, paper was already being used more frequently than parchment, and by the 16th century it had become the dominant material.[50]

The "mixed" use of parchment and paper, common until the 15th century, is also reflected in the surviving architectural drawings.

In 1419, Viennese stonemason Simon wrote in his will:

> *"My art on paper or parchment shall be given to my brother-in-law Helbling."*
>
> (Original in German: *"mein kunst in dem papir oder pyrmeid, die sol man geben meinem swager dem Helbling."*)[51]

From the years 1448/49 a drawing for the collegiate church of St. Waltrude in Mons near Bergen in Hainaut (Belgium) has been preserved. The upper part is drawn on parchment, while the lower part consists of three-ply strips of paper glued together. The watermark indicates that the paper was produced in northern France between 1375 and 1427.[52]

When Johannes Gutenberg introduced the printing press around 1450, he already had access to a reasonable amount of paper of the appropriate quality, although he still had to buy additional paper from abroad. One sixth of his 42-line Bible he printed in 1454 was still printed on parchment.[53] Printing technology spread as quickly as paper production, so that by 1500, just 50 years after Gutenberg's invention, there were some 1,000 printing houses in 250 locations in Europe.[54]

With the start of letterpress printing, the demand for paper grew exponentially, and quite a few printers maintained their own paper mills to meet their needs. But paper was always expensive and in short supply, despite the constant increase in production and the growing number of European mills. It was not until the 15th century that the price of paper plummeted massively: it cost only a tenth of the price of parchment, making it generally affordable and enabling its establishment in the first place.[55]

The reason for the persistent shortage was that sufficient quantities of raw materials, i. e. rags, could often not be obtained quickly enough for production. For several centuries, the authorities tried to counteract the shortage of raw materials by regulating the market (export bans, customs duties and rag allocation areas for certain mills), but a flourishing black market developed that undermined the official requirements for obtaining the coveted used textiles.[56] As a result, some paper mills were forced to close again due to the lack of raw materials.

It was not until the 18th century that people began experimenting with other raw materials for papermaking. When rags were finally replaced by wood fibers in the mid-19th century and machine production continued to improve as a result of industrialization, the supply crisis for writing materials finally came to an end.[57] Since then, paper has been *continuously* available in Europe as an *affordable* writing material.

The period for which architectural historians have identified a vacuum of construction plans corresponds quite precisely to the period in which there was a glaring shortage of writing materials in Europe. Papyrus was no longer available, parchment was extremely expensive and in some cases unsuitable for drawings due to its material properties, and paper was still unknown. Paper became widely used only in the 14th century and, as its price fell, from the 15th century onwards. It is precisely from this period that the number of plans increases noticeably.[58]

The medievalist François Bucher compiled 2,200 medieval European construction plans, including theoretical treatises and drawings; most of which date from 1350 to 1572.[59] Paul Booz confirmed that from the 15th century onward, not only did building plans increase *"in absolute number,"* but those on paper became *"a clear preponderance."* [60]

Max Hasak stated that the leakage of plans was less in western and southern Germany than in northern Germany, the region of the Brick Gothic.[61] This again is also consistent with the "travel direction" of the paper: Coming over the Alps from Italy, with which Upper German merchants had maintained intensive trade relations for centuries – especially with Venice and Genoa –, paper first reached the southwestern region in Germany with the important trading cities of Ravensburg, Nuremberg and Augsburg. These were the first to set up their own paper mills. In the north, on the other hand, paper was imported for a while via France, Bruges and Antwerp, until paper mills were also established in the Hanseatic region, for example in Lübeck starting in 1420. In the region of the the Brick Gothic, it was therefore initially much more difficult to get hold of paper than in southern Germany. This explains the late start of the plans in the north.

2.2 Literacy in Medieval Europe

Scriptureless because there was a lack of writing media

In my view, there is a close connection between literacy – the degree to which a population can read and write – and the availability of writing materials. In Greece, a literate culture developed from the 6th century B. C. onward, science, philosophy, and literature took off significantly. Many works that had been passed down orally were written down for the first time. Almost everyone in the population could now acquire the ability to read and write, as a fully developed alphabetic script (the Semitic-Phoenician alphabetic script) was already available. The 6th century B. C. is also the time when papyrus became established as a writing material in the European Mediterranean region.

Before that, it was only possible to "write" on stone or clay with great difficulty – or rather, it was very difficult to chisel characters with great effort, as the etymological root of the English word *write* (related to the German word "ritzen") attests. The original meaning of *write* as well as "ritzen" is "carve, engrave" or "scratch". Writing on papyrus, on the other hand, was easy, effortless, and did not require strength, given the appropriate quill and ink. Moreover, unlike stone and clay, papyrus as a writing material was light and easy to transport. The common papyrus format of the Greco-Roman period, with a height of 11.8 inches, roughly corresponds to the modern European DIN A4 format (210 x 297 mm) or the US standard letter format (8.5 x 11 in). Papyrus rolls allowed additional sheets to be glued on or cut off as needed, depending on the amount of text.[62] This made it possible for the first time to record longer written texts instead of short notes, and it inspired numerous authors to prepare books with larger page counts. Virtually all the major works of antiquity, including Vitruvius' *De architectura libri decem* ("Ten Books on Architecture"), were written on papyrus.

Even in the Middle Ages, there is a correlation between the degree of literacy and the availability of writing materials. A look at the literacy rates of the European population in the early and high Middle Ages shows the extent to which we can assume that master builders were able to read and write. Insightful scientific research by medievalists and Germanists, based on numerous sources, provides a fairly complete picture of the literacy of political rulers (nobles, kings and emperors), clergy, merchants and book authors. Literacy is defined here as the ability to use the written word as a means of communication.[63] Someone who can only write his name is therefore not considered literate.

By the 6th century A. D., literacy in Europe was at a high level. Many rulers were literate and signed documents independently; there were also professional scribes who transcribed books and documents, as well as organized private instruction.[64]

The ability to write slowly declined in Europe after the 7th century, and since the middle of the 9th century a real break seems to have occurred.[65] Remarkably, this period coincides with the decline of papyrus as writing material. In Italy, however, the ability to write was preserved to a greater extent than north of the Alps in France, Germany and England.

The lack of writing ability is documented, for example, by several rulers who were no longer able to sign documents after about 750. Charles the Great (747 – 814), his brother Carloman and his father Pippin (714 – 768) were unable to write. Instead of a signature, they simply placed the execution line in a monogram drawn by a scribe under a document. The inability of rulers to write contributed to the increasing use of seals to replace signatures on documents north of the Alps.[66] There was no longer any public transmission of knowledge, and the educational institutions that had existed since antiquity disappeared.

In the period between Louis the German (806 – 876) and Charles IV (1316 – 78), few secular and ecclesiastical rulers seem to have been literate.[67] Frederick Barbarossa (1122 – 90) seems, at best, to have learned to read a little in his old age, while his second wife Beatrice was considered literate. Even Ruprecht I Elector Palantine, who founded the University of Heidelberg in 1386, was illiterate. When Nicolas of Cusa proposed a secret and written election of the Roman king in 1433, the electors had to be allowed to bring secretaries, since not all of them were literate. It was not until the second half of the 14th century that rulers became increasingly literate again, and since Maximilian I (1459 – 1519) all German emperors could write and read again.[68] Thus, literacy resumed at the very time when paper had become established in Central Europe.

The same applies to the clergy as to the nobility. By no means all clerics were literate, although the clergy had a monopoly on education in the early and high Middle Ages, and it was in the monasteries where books were eagerly reproduced in order to increase the book stock. It is documented, for example, that in the middle of the 13th century there were illiterate abbots and prelates in Romagna, Auvergne, Sardinia and Corsica. In 1291, in the Provostry of Lucerne (Switzerland) and in the Monastery of Murbach (Germany), the provost, the abbot and three monks could not sign a contract of sale. In St. Gall – a monastery that was considered particularly progressive and for which, as is known, the famous St. Gall monastery plan (cf. Figure 1) had been drawn up around 825 – the abbot, the provost and nine monks of the monastery could not sign a deed of conferral in 1291.[69]

In a Benedictine abbey near Nice in 1320, 16 out of 18 monks declared that they could not write, including priests, for whom the church itself required literacy as prerequisite for their profession. Nevertheless, in Italy, France, England and in the German-speaking world, even bishops who could not write can be traced back to the 13th century, e. g. Archbishop Frederick II of Salzburg (1270 – 84). Canon law prohibited the "illiterates" from entering the clerical state, but this seems to have meant only the ability to read, not to write. It was therefore sufficient for a cleric to be able to read, especially Latin, since in early Europe every document was written in Latin and not in the vernacular language. Reading and writing were apparently taught and learned separately.[70]

In European cities, urban Latin schools were introduced only in the second half of the 13th century, for example in Lübeck in 1262 and in Breslau in 1267, but the introduction of compulsory education was a long time coming. Estimates based on sources suggest that in the 15th century only 3 to 4 percent of the total population could write. By 1600, even at the University of Vienna not all students knew how to write.[71] Compulsory education was introduced in Germany in Saxe-Coburg-Gotha in 1642, in Württemberg in 1649, in Brandenburg in 1662 and in Prussia in 1717/36. As a result, the number of literate people rose to between 10 and 25 percent of the population in the 17th and 18th centuries.[72]

The situation was no different in the other Central European countries: In France, 53 percent of the enlisted soldiers were illiterate in 1831, a figure that dropped to 37 percent by 1854. In England, one-third of men and half of women were illiterate in 1840.[73] The rapid decline of illiteracy and the widespread literacy of the population in Europe occurred between 1830 and 1890, and continued until about 1910.

It is evident that the literacy rate of master builders or architects must have corresponded to the average of the population. Paul Booz has collected some sources that provide information on the literacy of architects. Even from the 14th to 16th centuries, illiterate builders are known by name, e. g. Hieronymus Lotter (1497 – 1580), the builder of the Augustusburg in Leipzig (Germany).

In the 16th century, Johann Neudörfer, a master scribe and arithmetician from Nuremberg, stated that a certain

> *"(carpenter) Weber can neither write nor read. Nevertheless, regarding the proportion of the wheels, and all sorts of millwork, he is so excellent that he lacks nothing with regard to number and measure."*
>
> (Original in German: *"(Zimmermeister) Weber weder schreiben noch lesen kann, so ist er doch in der Proportion der Räder, in allerhand Mühlwerk so fürtrefflich, dass ihm an Zahl und Maß garnichts mangelt und abgeht.")*[74]

Similar to the political rulers, the city of Vienna, as late as 1637, allowed its master stonemasons and bricklayers, who were unable to read or write, to have their signatures made by a scribe as a substitute.[75]

It was a long way from preliteracy to the continuous literacy in Europe, which lasted from the introduction of paper in the 14th century until the late 19th century. If illiterate master builders were common until the early 17th century, it can be concluded that between the 6th and 13th/14th centuries architects – like the rest of the population – were predominantly or almost exclusively illiterate with regard to their writing and reading skills.

And even if someone was literate, this did not yet mean that he could read books, because until the 15th century books were consistently written in Latin. It was only with the introduction of letterpress printing that the vernacular languages of each country gradually began to prevail in written documents.

"Shoes made of lead" – papers replace personal presence

The introduction of paper fundamentally changed culture in Europe – as it had done before in the Arab world and in China: Personal presence could now be replaced by papers of various kinds. On the political level, the advantages of written documentation of deeds, decrees, laws, etc. were quickly recognized. They saved the nobility the time-consuming traveling around their respective domains. The increase in written correspondence led to the end of the so-called "itinerant court". Rulers settled down in a permanent central residence instead of moving from palatinate to palatinate. Instead of appearing in person, they sent a messenger to deliver the appropriate paper.

Thus, beginning around 1250 and intensifying since the 14th century, the development of the written form accelerated in the sovereign and municipal chanceries, especially in the commercial cities. The output of documents increased, and gradually a (bureaucratic) administration developed that functioned with the help of an apparatus of secretaries or scribes:[76]

> *"Where nobility cannot travel, it mobilizes letters or manuscripts that break the fixed bond between the person and his place. [...] The text carried by the voice depends on the immediate situational conditions, on the range of sensory perception that determines any oral communication. The use of scripts*

> *makes it possible to see more than the eyes allow, and to hear farther than one's ears can manage, to participate in situations and circumstances that exceed physical possibilities."*[77]

In the early 13th century major trading cities also began to establish what we would call now "munipical administration" in the early 13th century: Cologne, the largest city in Germany at the time, was the first to appoint an official scribe in 1228 and began documenting a small portion of the city's operations in a written form in the so-called "Schreinsbücher" (i. e. books kept in a special chest). Within about 80 to 100 years, most of the German cities followed suit, such as Strasbourg in 1233, Würzburg in 1236, Regensburg, Neuss and Lübeck in 1242, Hamburg in 1259, Rostock in 1257, Wismar in 1260, Augsburg in 1268, Erfurt in 1265, Hanover in 1301, and so on.[78] Once introduced, the city administrations quickly expanded, and soon the number of scribes in larger cities increased from two to five.

The same advantage, namely replacing personal presence with written documents, was also recognized by the European long-distance merchants, who were the first to come into contact with the new writing material "paper" as a commodity. While they initially took clergymen with them as scribes on their journeys, it was they who learned to write and calculate earlier and faster than the rest of the population. From the early 13th century[79], European merchants used a variety of papers to facilitate commercial contacts, business transactions and payments. Transporting and selling goods over long distances were always associated with high risks: Thieves, highwaymen, robber barons and pirates threatened merchants and their cargoes on long voyages, often lasting months, during which they could lose their entire stock of goods as well as their money (and their lives).

"Papers" significantly reduced the risk:

- Checks and bills of exchange largely eliminated the need to carry cash.

- Waybills, delivery bills and invoices made it unmistakably clear which goods had been sold to whom and at what price.
- Loan contracts governed the liabilities between the capital provider and the capital borrower.
- Insurance and notarization helped reduce the risk, especially of shipments.
- Letters supported communication with trading posts often thousands of miles away.
- Continuously kept business books provided an overview of the entire flow of goods and money over time and space.

In the 13th and 14th centuries, most long-distance merchants no longer traveled themselves, but set up factories at their various trading posts, which were run by factors – in modern terms: managing directors with procuration – and with whom they were in close contact by letter. The merchants themselves settled down and operated from their home bases.[80] The well-known Italian merchant Francesco Datini (c. 1335 – 1410) from Prato was the source of no less than 150,000 written documents including about 11,000 letters on paper, which were discovered in the 20th century.[81] Addressing one of his agents, Datini recommends:

> *"May you take care of the company's affairs in shoes made of lead."* [82]

This means: The merchant could "nail" his legs to the desk and conduct business exclusively from his office – his "writing chamber", *scriverecamere*, his kontor. This not only reduced the risk of long journeys, but also saved a lot of time, not to mention bookkeeping and balance sheets: The Franciscan friar Luca Paccioli developed double-entry bookkeeping in 1494, which was very quickly adopted by merchants. However, almost two centuries earlier, merchants started to keep business books and establish accounting.

Thus, business books from Nuremberg are already known from the years 1304 to 1307.[83]

Early on, merchants pushed for their children to be educated in special schools that were distinctly different from the "Latin schools" with their more religious and clerical orientation. In these schools the children were to be taught the necessary commercial knowledge. As early as 1262, for example, a separate school for merchants' children was founded in Lübeck at St. Jakobi, which was no longer exclusively in the hands of the church.[84] For several centuries, it was also common for self-respecting German merchants to send their children to Italy in order to receive a commercial education.

The increase in speed resulting from the use of written documents instead of personal presence led to an intensification of long-distance trade from the 14th century onwards, which in turn favored the cultural and economic upswing of Europe and soon led to the Renaissance of the 15th and 16th centuries. However, it must be explicitly emphasized that the advance of the use of paper and written documents affected only the long-distance merchants, who mainly fulfilled the function of wholesalers, but not the grocers or retailers, who sold their goods only at their place of residence. Other professions and segments of the population were equally unaffected.

Early pioneers who used the form of writing, were politicians and long-distance merchants. They were the first to recognize that written documents could replace personal presence, relieve the burden on memory, speed up processes, and make them more secure.

2.3 Preliterate cultures think differently – or: why the horse is not a "secret car"

Literacy as a catalyst of cultural development

Prior to the 13th and 14th centuries, Europe was what linguists call an "oral culture", that is, a culture that did not use the written form, but communicated primarily orally through personal communication. More precisely, Europe was not so much an "oral" as a "preliterate" culture, since writing had never completely disappeared since antiquity, but remained in the form of "islands", the monasteries and the clergy, and as a craft of professional scribes (mostly of clerical origin) who could be hired when needed.

In contrast to other cultures that had no scripture at all and were completely illiterate, Europe was not entirely unfamiliar with written documents, although literacy had declined sharply since the 8th century. Surprisingly, it took six centuries after the introduction of paper, roughly from the 14th to the late 19th century, for literacy to spread throughout Central Europe. Nowadays, we take it so much for granted that everyone can write and read that we give no thought to what a world without written texts might look like. Rather, we assume that oral or preliterate cultures "function" just like our culture.

But the linguistic and communication research of recent decades has shown that the differences in the understanding of the world between oral / preliterate and literate cultures are enormous. Cultures without a

written language cannot be understood if presuppositions are imposed on them that do not apply to them. Oral and literate cultures are so fundamentally diffefrent in their way of thinking and acting that, in fact, communication between the two is indeed difficult, sometimes impossible.

The communication researcher Walter Ong has used an apt comparison to show how difficult it is for us fully literate people in the Western world today to understand the thinking and the actions of people of an oral (or preliterate) culture.[85] From the point of view of a car as today's means of transportation, it is as if one were to describe the horse as an earlier means of transportation. According to this, a horse would be a "car without wheels, engine and steering wheel". If you only know cars and have never seen a horse, you will wonder how it can move at all, because it lacks – from today's point of view – everything that is essential for a means of transportation.

It is precisely this view that is applied to the master builders of the early and high Middle Ages when architectural and art historians assert that the complex church buildings of the Romanesque and Gothic periods could only have been erected with the help of exact and complete construction plans – and this for the sole reason that today all buildings are erected exclusively in this way.

Oral and literate cultures differ not only in the spread of literacy, but even more widely: people in oral cultures have a completely different way of thinking and acting, different organizational structures, and even a different functioning of legal and political systems. We make the mistake of imagining the oral world of thought and communication as a *"variant of the literate world we know"* [86] and of believing that writing merely represents language in visible form.[87] But a literate culture is not an "oral culture plus the written form" but a *different*, distinct culture. It would go beyond the scope of this book and its subject to list all the differences between the two forms of culture, so in this context, I will highlight only a few key differences that must have had an impact on the art of building, as they had an impact on society as a whole.

To people who cannot read or write, texts often seem like *magic*, almost like a fetish. This has been demonstrated in different cultures around the world, and there are clear traces of it in the European Middle Ages. Writing was, especially for illiterates, a kind of "sacred act" of monks and church people who were able to do. The written parchment as a result of this act was the "sacred text". This was expressed, for example, in the fact that in the 11th century, written texts were kept in reliquaries or sacristies, right next to the bones of the saints. It was only with the advent of the flood of written documents that this practice was abondoned.[88]

In the Middle Ages, land transfers in the form of deeds were difficult because it had to be made clear to the parties concerned that the change of ownership was based exclusively on a piece of parchment, a deed, and that this was legally binding, even if one or both of the parties involved could not read the deed. Quasi-magical rituals were used, in which the reading of the text was dispensable for the transfer of ownership.[89] For example, a clod of earth, a sword, or some other object was ceremonially placed on a Bible or a gospel book as part of the land to be granted. Or the document itself had to be touched with the hand in order to make the contract legally binding. Sometimes the symbolic object along with the document was displayed on an altar for a longer period of time to demonstrate the change in ownership.[90]

A remarkable light is shed on the early handling of written documents by the following incident: After the death of an archbishop in England in the late 8th century, the ecclesiastical deed to a monastery was stolen by a king, who immediately claimed ownership of it based on the document. However, it was not the king, but someone else who was named as the legal new owner in the document.[91] According to this, the king could not read the deed at all. This shows that the written paper was treated as a fetish: The possession of the document as such – regardless of its content – is attributed magical powers. We may smile at this naivety today, but it shows how people being ignorant of writing and reading dealt with written documents and how they regarded them. And it also sheds light on the fact that a culture first has to slowly get used to writing things down and learn how to deal with the written form.

What might illiterate architects of the early Middle Ages have thought about deeds, documents and other written materials? There are no surviving answers to this question, but it can be assumed that they regarded them like the rest of the population. Plans certainly had much less importance for them than we attach to them nowadays. It is known that people in oral or preliterate cultures live strongly in the here and now and are much less oriented to the past and future than we are, because they cannot measure time. Their sense of time and action is more focused on the present.

The habit of writing down facts only began with the establishment of writing as a cultural technique and the fact that, over time, more and more of social life was regulated by written documents rather than by oral agreement, personal presence, and action in the here and now. Communication researchers Ivan Illich and Barry Sanders state:

> *"In the part of the world that lies north of the Alps, an unprecedented change in the nature of social relations took place between the middle of the 12th century and the end of the 13th century: Trust, power, property, and all the concerns of everyday life were henceforth functions of the alphabet. The use of documents, accompanied by a new way of designing the written*

page, transformed writing, which in the early and high Middle Ages had been praised and venerated as a mysterious figuration of the Word of God, into an essential part of the mediation of worldly relations." [92]

It is precisely during this period of fundamental change in European culture from a preliterate to a literate one that the first architectural drawings on parchment appeared (cf. section 3.1)

From memory to the written record

Another characteristic feature of oral or preliterate cultures is that people have a much more developed memory than in literate cultures, which outsource their memory to paper. In order to preserve their knowledge, they devote a great deal of energy to constant repetition, usually through orally reciting bards and poets,[93] but also by means of multiple "rebuilding and copying" of buildings, as evidenced in the Arab world (cf. section 2.5).

Members of oral or preliterate cultures can remember complex facts and relationships to an extent that we can hardly imagine. Therefore, it seems self-evident that master builders could think up complex buildings and keep all the necessary details in mind.

This is acknowledged now and then by architectural historians like Paul Booz who states:

"The old masters had the astonishing ability to conceive even extensive buildings in their minds, i. e. to develop them directly on the building site without the mediation of a draft. Needless to say that this required a great deal of practice and experience as well as considerable spatial imagination." [94]

The phrase that a building was "conceived in the mind" *(opus in mente conceptum) is often* found in medieval literature.[95] For example, Robert Grosseteste (c. 1175–1253), philosopher and Bishop of Lincoln, states:

> *"Imagine, then, in the mind of the artifisan the form of the [work of] art that is to be created, as, for example, in the mind of the master builder the form and likeness of the house that is to be built. He refers only to the form and likeness in order to build the house in imitation of it. [...] Thus, in the way in which the form of the house would correspond to its form in the mind of such a master builder, the artistry of Almighty God, whether wisdom or word, is the form of all created beings."* [96]

Similar statements can already be found in Vitruvius, Boethius and Augustine. William of Auvergne (c. 1180 – 1249), theologian and bishop of Paris, mentioned for the first time that it was useful to make a drawing between the mental conception and the execution, if only for mnemotechnical reasons, not as a binding construction plan in the modern sense:

> *"[...] Therefore, when he imagines the model of any such a thing, he should meanwhile externally, so that it does not escape from his heart through forgetfulness, make its description by notes and formations, to which he should return as often as he realizes that he has forgotten something of what he had previously thought."* [97]

In Wilhelm's remarks, we see the gradual transition from a preliterate to literate culture: written records are already supported, but at first they serve only as aids to memory before fulfilling more comprehensive tasks.

It seems like "magic" to us today to develop a complex building directly on site and to keep the overall planning in mind, even over several generations of architects or several decades or centuries. But for medieval master builders, at least until the middle of the 13th

century, this was quite common and had become a routine due to their illiteracy and excellent memory. As members of a literate culture we have elevated paper to a storage medium for the past and the future, we can remember much less, and therefore assume that even the master builders had to plan complex buildings in advance with the help of drawings. This is like looking for the engine, steering wheel and wheels of a horse – to use Walter Ong's metaphor – because we only know the car.

People in oral or preliterate cultures think in situational, operational frames of reference, not abstract ones. It is the written form that separates the knower from the substance of knowledge and establishes a kind of "objective" separation or personal disengagement between the two.[98] Moreover, people of oral or preliterate cultures think additively rather than subordinately. That is, they tend to arrange facts in terms of their equivalents, without paying attention to superordinate or subordinate categories or opposites. This can be observed in their use of language. Their speech is redundant to a greater extent than we are accustomed to with written material, so that it appears to us to be prolix and long-winded; this presumably serves to improve memorability.[99]

The fact that members of an oral culture do not record anything in written form does not necessarily mean that they know or can do "less" than members of literate cultures, but that they think and act "differently". Illiteracy is often subject to negative evaluations in a literate culture like ours. But we should regard it without judgement:

> *"Oral cultures produce [...] powerful and beautiful [...] expressions of high artistic and human value,"* according to the communications researcher Walter Ong.[100]

Anyone familiar with Romanesque and Gothic church buildings will readily agree.

Literate cultures differ from oral and preliterate cultures not only in their reliance on writing, but also in the way they organize their entire social life. Before the written form is established as a unifying element of communication, oral or preliterate cultures go through several stages: In the first stage, they still perceive the act of writing and the written documents themselves as "magical" or "sacred", in the second stage they initially concede to them merely the function of a memory aid, and in the third stage, a cultural transformation sets in, through which written texts become the supporting pillar of social interaction.

2.4 Villard de Honnecourt, role model for the development of construction and engineering technology

On the threshold of literate culture

Let's take a look at the writing and reading skills of one of the most outstanding architectural engineers of the early and high Middle Ages. Here, too, some surprises await us. Villard de Honnecourt (around 1200 – 50) was a kind of pioneer of his time with his famous Sketchbook ("Album of Drawing and Sketches", original in French: *Album de dessins et croquis*). Even today, in the absence of other sketches, his architectural drawings are often referred to by historians to reconstruct the work of Gothic master builders.

The work of Villard de Honnecourt, created around 1235, was still entirely written on parchment of varying quality: he used smoother, higher-quality parchment for particularly beautiful figures, and rougher for technical drawings.[101] He also lacked space on his sheets. He was noticeably economical with the available and expensive writing material, sometimes placing very different drawings on one and the same page of parchment. The work was created about five to six decades before paper began to spread from Italy to Central Europe on a significant scale. Villard had worked in various Gothic workshops (Bauhütten) and probably spent his apprenticeship at the Cistercian Abbey of Vaucelles.

Nowadays, his Sketchbook appears to us like a "hogdepodge" of the most diverse drawings that have no system, no recognizable order, and refer to very different subjects in construction, engineering as well as medicine. In addition to advice and recipes for scarring wounds, there are schematic drawings of animals and humans, drawings of engineering performance such as a water-powered saw, but also incomplete floor plan drawings of cathedrals, for example of Laôn and Reims.

This seems strange to a modern reader, living in a thoroughly literate culture like ours. We cannot explain why such heterogeneous drawings are united in one book. A comprehensible explanation is provided by Günther Binding and Norbert Nussbaum, according to whom Villard's work is a notebook and workbook in the tradition of a Piccardian construction workshop (Bauhütte); in the manner of a compendium, it documents the knowledge and skill of the workshop or the architect.[102]

Typical of oral or preliterate cultures, Villard took an additive rather than a subordinating approach to content: He simply lined up different topics one after the other, without any structuring superordination or subordination, which is undoubtedly what we would choose today if we had to organize a larger amount of material.

Villard was an early representative of the European literate culture – one who lived and worked on the epochal threshold from the preliterate to the literate world. In addition to the incompleteness of the work, of which only about half has survived, one reason for the juxtaposition of content may be that coherent text structures first became established with the printing of books. The text composition that concentrates on one theme and unfolds it step by step is the achievement of a developed literate culture.

The preface to his Sketchbook is remarkable, in which Villard introduces himself and his work with the following words in Old French, mixed with Latin elements, on plate 2 (fol. 1v):

> *"Villard de Honnecourt salutes you and prays that all those who will work with the devices found in this book will pray for his*

soul and remember him. For in this book one can find sound advice on the techniques of masonry and on the devices of carpentry. And, likewise, you will find the techniques of representation, which is characterized as the discipline of geometry, which commands and instructs it." [103]

(Original in French: *"Wilars de Honecourt v(os) salue (et) si proie a tos ceus qui de ces engiens ouverront, c'on trovera en cest livre q(u)'il proient por s'arme (et) qu'il lor soviengne de lui. Car en cest livre puet o(n) trover grant consel de la grant force de maconerie (et) den engiens de carpenterie, (et) si troveres de force de la portraiture, le trais, ensi come li ars de iometrie le (com)ma(n) d(e) (et) ensaigne.")*[104]

The introduction to the Sketchbook has two features characteristic of the epochal threshold from preliterate to literate culture:

- The reader is greeted – including the religious reference that was certainly common at that time – and addressed personally, as someone who stands physically in front of the author and to whom the author talks but does not write for. An author of the early 13th century could not imagine a "distant" reader reading the text in another place and time, possibly centuries later. The experience of a voice and the reading of books could not yet be consistently distinguished. Books imitated the situation of spoken language, of dialogue.[105] Early works of written culture always imitated the forms of the preceding oral culture until independent literary text structures emerged.
- The author speaks of himself in the third person, calling himself *"Wilars de Honecourt"*, just as if he wanted to introduce another person present in addition to his "interlocutor", the reader, and himself. The "writing self", who introduces himself as author in the text with "I" or sometimes with "we," becomes common at a later stage of a more elaborate literacy. The self as a social construct and the text

developed on each other over two to three centuries until there was finally an "author" as the originator of the text.[106]

Villard's last sentence is especially noteworthy: *"You will find the techniques of representation, which the features as the discipline of geometry commands and instructs it"*. Two things become clear from this important sentence:

- Villard seems to have regarded his work as a kind of textbook (French: *"enseigner" = "teaching")* for other architects and engineers.
- And, more importantly: Apparently, the knowledge of how to draw geometric models and plans was not yet part of the usual know-how of his time, because otherwise Villard's drawings would have been superfluous. It would have made little sense to publish "trivial" knowledge and tools that were available to everyone as a matter of course.

This, in turn, suggests that the builders of the early Middle Ages were not thoroughly familiar with model and plan drawing. Thinking and constructing "according to plan" and with the help of calculations corresponds to a literate culture, not an oral one.

Villard may have sensed how difficult it was for his contemporaries to understand his designs. On the pages dealing with geometric squaring, he uses the term "geometry" several times, repeating it, for example, on plate 39 (fol. 20r):

> *"All of these figures are geometrical representations."* (French original: *"Totes ces figures sunt estraites de geometrie.")*[107]

This sentence is framed at the bottom right of plate 39 of his work, shown below (cf. Figure 6). Conrad finds fault with this plate, again from the point of view of an author who belongs to today's literate culture:

> *"The accompanying texts are concise and could have used more explanatory words if knowledge was to be imparted."*[108]

Conrad may have understood this as an objection to the fact that the Sketchbook could not have been a "textbook" in the sense of a school book. But in Villard's time, there was no "standard" for textbooks in which text and images were coordinated in such a way that students would have had an optimal learning template. The question remains open whether Villard wrote his work for future master builders, for the apprentices of a particular (his?) workshop (Bauhütte), and / or for a larger reading public. The personal presentation of the author in words and pictures speaks for the latter.

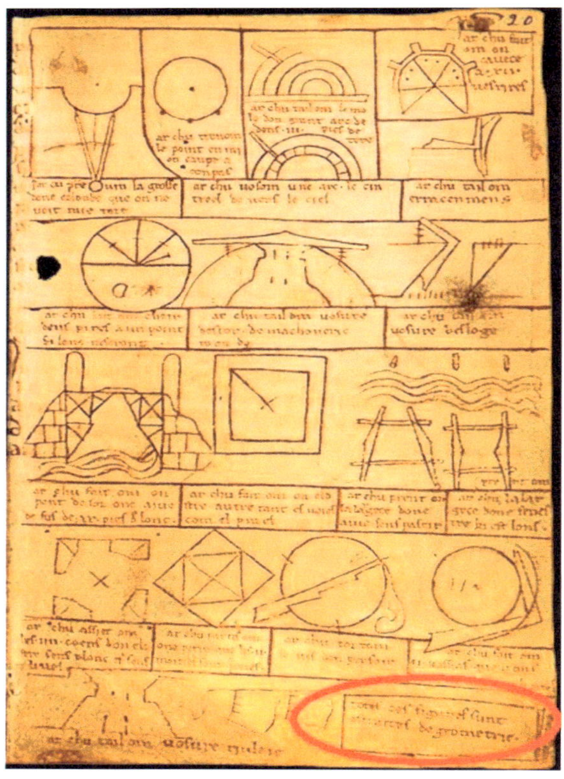

Figure 6: Plate 39 from Villard de Honnecourt's *Album de dessins et croquis* ("Album of Drawing and Sketches"). Framed at the bottom right is the sentence: "Totes ces figures sunt estraites de geometrie."

It is clearly recognizable that the texts were written around Villard's drawings without a recognizable layout, i. e., they were inserted afterwards. In addition, his drawings are "crisscrossed" in different reading directions often on a single plate or sheet – probably to save expensive parchment.

Was Villard an architect at all?

Some experts, such as Carl F. Barnes and George Brooks, doubt that Villard was a master builder at all. Barnes does not consider him an architect because his Sketchbook does not contain *complete overall plans.* Also, the variety of subjects he covered would argue against this. He considers him a skilled metal worker. His small drawings would indicate that he was not familiar with designing buildings on a large scale.[109] Brooks feels similarly:

> *"Villard could not have been an architect – nor was he any sort of mason – but he must have been more than an artist, more technically minded than a dilettante, and certainly more than a clerk."* [110]

Therefore, he assumes that he was a carpenter. He justifies this as follows:

- His Sketchbook contained numerous illustrations of wooden machines, such as a saw driven by a water wheel.
- His few drawings of architectural building elements were never realized, but were made freely and imprecisely in comparison with the originals.
- His name as an architect has not been handed down for any building.
- His drawings of wooden objects are clearly more precise than those of stone components.
- He was familiar with the techniques of carpentry and mechanical engineering.[111]

All this is true, and yet it does not contradict the fact that Villard could have been an architect because in the Middle Ages there was no separation between the profession of architect and the profession of engineer. This specialization developed in the 18th century, that is, in the Baroque period; it arose from the need to calculate the trajectories of cannonballs and fortress walls.[112] In the Middle Ages, however, it was common for the architect of a building to also be responsible for the manufacture of the mechanical or wooden machinery needed to erect the structure, such as hoists and tread wheels. And an architect was not always a skilled stonemason or mason; he might have learned the carpentry trade as well. Moreover, only a few architects have survived by name from the early 13th century. It was not until the 14th century that this changed.

Barnes and Brooks apply inappropriate standards to Villard's Sketchbook by comparing it to the work of modern architects and modern construction plans. In this way, they treat the "horse" as a "secret, undiscovered car" and can only conclude that Villard could *not* have been an architect.

Sketchbooks like Villard's continued to be produced by master builders for their work several centuries later. The architect Hans Hammer (also known as "Hans Meiger of Werde," c. 1440 – 1519), for example, produced a voluminous "pattern book" around 1480/81. It shows strong structural similarities to Villard's Sketchbook, as it also addresses a variety of different topics. Hans Hammer sketched, among other things, numerous lifting machines, cranes, coats of arms, protractors, sundials, various winches and pulleys, spiral staircases, pointed arches, vault forms, finials, pier cross-sections, floor plan elements and other components (cf. Figure 7).[113] He drew from concrete models of existing buildings and varied them, as Villard also seems to have done. In addition, there are handwritten notes of several pages that are not found in Villard's work; this shows that Hans Hammer was literate, typical of the late 15th century, when literacy was on the rise (cf. section 3.1). However, general construction plans are just as absent from his notebook as they are from Villard's.

If one were to infer Hans Hammer's profession from the variety of subjects in the pattern book, the imprecision and quantity of the architectural drawings, and the large number of wooden machines, one might also question whether he was an architect and consider him to be a carpenter. However, he was undoubtedly the master architect of Strasbourg Cathedral from 1486 to 1490/92 and from 1510 to 1519, where he created, among other things, the pulpit in the flamboyant late Gothic style, and he also worked as an architect on other churches.[114]

Notebooks, sketchbooks, or pattern books such as Villard de Honnecourt's seem to have been frequently used by architects for their work since the early Middle Ages, although only a few have survived. They probably served as aids to memory and design in daily work, and possibly also for the training of apprentices and journeymen. However, the contents were probably not usually implemented 1:1. The fact that (overall) construction plans in the modern style are missing in them does not allow any conclusions to be drawn about the profession or professionalism of the draftsman. Villard de Honnecourt, unlike Hans Hammer, seems to have prepared his sketchbook for a later publication by the texts he inserted afterwards.

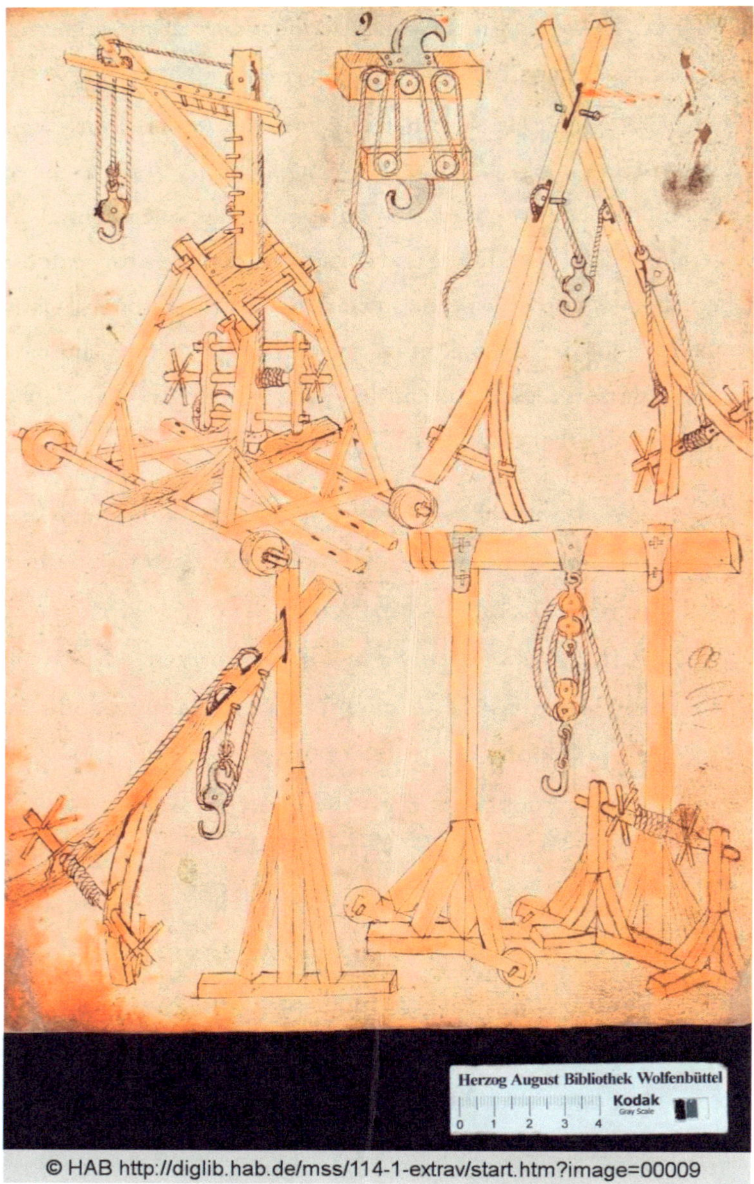

Figure 7: Wooden machines (lifting gears) from the unpublished, privately made and used notebook of the Strasbourg master builder Hans Hammer (= Hans Meiger of Werde), created around 1480/81.

How geometry is perceived by illiterates

Back to Villard in the 13th century: Villard's statement that his drawings are *"geometric illustrations"* seems self-evident to us and would be confirmed by any ten-year-old child today, but it was by no means so to his contemporaries, otherwise he would not have mentioned it explicitly and several times. What shines through in his work are the beginnings of the application of geometry and the construction of a three-dimensional structure on a two-dimensional surface.

The modern architect or structural engineer will now ask himself in amazement: The master builders of the Middle Ages quite obviously used geometry in their construction, even if they were not supposed to have written plans – why should they not have known that it was "geometry"? This is another question posed from the point of view of a literate culture. In their daily practice, the builders applied something for which they must not have known the name, the designation. This is typical of oral or preliterate cultures, which do not possess categories of analytical thought that could structure knowledge from a distance to lived experience.[115]

It is possible that master builders were unfamiliar with the designations of geometric figures, that they simply had "no words" for what they used every day, and that they did not know the technical terms invented by scholars and already known to some extent in the Middle Ages, especially since they were mostly expressed in Latin. One can imagine this as being similar to children, who can laugh heartily at a joke even before they have terms like "joke," "humor", or "comedy" in their active vocabulary.

> *"An oral culture is simply not concerned with [...] abstract categories, formal logical thought processes, definitions, or even thorough descriptions, not with dissected self-analysis, which always comes not simply from thinking, but from textual thinking",*[116] according to the communication researcher Walter Ong.

For members of an oral culture, "words" have the character of concrete "events" or "actions" and exude a "power-movement" that is tied to personal experience as well as to sound.[117] For members of literate cultures, on the other hand, words seem to be connected in a superficial way to "external things" that no longer have any power of their own, but are rather "dead objects". In literate cultures, words have the character of defined "thought constructs" that are often sharply delineated from one another, but above all do not represent actions or events, but are primarily "knowledge stuff".

In the literate culture, words are essentially *frozen* actions or events. This is reflected in Villard's statement *"This is called geometry"*: For him, geometry is the result of a drawing act. Jens Rüffer points out that Villard writes of an *"ars de iometrie"*, i. e. an *"art of geometry"*, and that the word *"ars"* refers to practical application, not to mathematical principles.[118]

According to Binding, "geometry" is understood by Vitruvius, Villard, and the medieval master builders as a practical "drawing and measuring aid" as it was handed down from antiquity by the agrimensors, the field surveyors.[119]

How book authors wrote texts in the Middle Ages

Under the title "Was Villard de Honnecourt illiterate?", a remarkable article was published in 1999 by the art historian Wilhelm Schlink. He referred to a much older article written by the philologist Friedrich Schneegans (1901), who had already noticed "inconsistencies" in Villard's work, i. e. with regard to language variants in the text. Schneegans had noted that Villard's text must apparently have been written by different scribes:

> *"Confusing are the multitude of scribal hands and the sometimes almost literal repetitions of legends in different script and orthography. Since Schneegans' philological investigation [...] it is considered certain that three scribes were at work."*[120]

On the other hand, there is no doubt that the drawings were *"made by the hand of a single author"*.[121] One of the scribes could have been Villard himself; two other scribes later added short explanatory texts, either on Villard's instructions as an author for his readers (possibly apprentices or journeymen of a lodge) or as his students for their own use.[122]

After discussing various aspects of the textual elements or legends present in Villard's work, which contain several repetitions, Schlink concluded:

> *"If Villard de Honnecourt had been illiterate – all problems of legend repetition would have been solved."*[123]

Schlink expressed disbelief in his thesis himself, particularly since Villard must have learned Latin in the monastery. Nonetheless, I concur that it may be correct since Villard was a typical author of his time.

In the early days of literate Europe, when only a small minority could read and write, a "craft literacy" initially developed. Scribes practiced writing like a trade or service and were assigned to write letters, documents or even books for a fee.[124] In modern terms, these scribes were "secretaries" who produced a text according to the author's dictation.

"(Book) authors" and "scribes" were usually not identical in the early and high Middle Ages. Even though authors could often read, it was commonplace for them to lack the ability to write. They dictated the text

> **to a scribe. The scribe was the *amanuensis*, the "one who goes to hand" or "henchman". The concept of an *au(c)tor* or "author" of a text was not established until the 14th century, starting with Bonaventure.[125]**

As it is well documented, several authors during the Middle Ages did not personally pen their work. Hildegard of Bingen (1098 – 1179), for example, dictated her books, which are still available in bookstore today, to writing experts in the monastery. Bernard of Clairvaux[126] (1090 – 1153) and even Oswald von Wolkenstein from the early 15th century (1377 – 1445) employed this method.[127] The poet Wolfram von Eschenbach (c. 1170 – 1237) openly admitted: *"All the reading is unknown to me, as it is known to others."*[128]

The personal separation of author and scribe is attested by numerous illustrations from the Middle Ages. For example, drawings from Hildegard of Bingen's works have survived showing her dictating to a monk and receiving a divine revelation, symbolized by flames above her head.

Additionally, an account of Rudolf von Ems (c. 1200 – 54), a contemporary of Villard de Honnecourt, with almost identical life data provides further insight. As an author, Rudolf created an extensive literary output including several stories as well as a "world chronicle".[129] In his works, he portrayed himself as the author, alongside his scribe. Rudolf holds a banner in his hand, which, in medieval illustrations, signifies that he delivers an oral lecture[130] – in modern terms it corresponds to the "speech bubble" that we still use today in comics or caricatures. His scribe sits to his right or in front of him with a book or folded sheet of paper with lines, where he records the dictated text.

Notker I of St. Gall (also called "Notker Balbulus", "Notker the Stammerer", c. 840 – 912) works as a poet, writer of documents and teacher at the monastery school. Unlike many of his contemporaries, he was able to write. In the illustration below (cf. Figure 8), he holds a quill in his left hand and an eraser in his right, a typical image of scribes in the Middle Ages. (He could have been left-handed since the typical positioning of quill and knife is reversed). The knife is used for scraping out mistakes made on parchment – which cannot be accomplished on paper – and to sharpen the quill. The eraser was also often used to flatten the parchment sheet to prevent it from wrinkling while applying ink and avoid getting fingerprints on it.

Figure 8: Notker I, called "Balbulus", "the Stammerer", scholar of St. Gall, at his writing desk – typical illustration of an author with quill and eraser (representation from the 11th century).

Portraits of authors, possibly along with their scribes, are found in many early works of the Middle Ages. This unmistakably expresses: "Look here, dear reader, this is me, the author, (and this is my scribe, who wrote my book according to my speech). This is how I (or we both) look like, and this is how this book came into being." Illustrations like this are the pictorial counterpart to the verbal greeting Villard uses at the beginning of his work.

Villard probably depicted himself pictorially in his work, too, which is located near the introductory greetings. His Sketchbook contains a drawing of a man (cf. Figure 9), generally interpreted as a self-portrait of the author. He raises his hand as if to greet the reader using a picture in addition to the introductory text.

Figure 9: Plate 3 from Villard de Honnecourt's *Album de dessins et croquis* ("Album of Drawings and Sketches"). Right next to the verbal greeting to the reader, there is a figure to be found without legend. It is probably the author himself who figuratively emphasizes the greeting to the reader with a gesture of his right hand. The only strange thing is that the figure looks like a knight or soldier (chain mail, shield and headgear).

Just as the author could not imagine a reading audience separated from him in time and space, readers could not imagine the creation of a book by an author separated in time and space.

The location of man in the space-time structure

Generally speaking, in the early days of literate culture it was not customary to place oneself in an "objective" space-time structure independent of one's own person, as we take for granted today. Thus, for example, early medieval documents that recorded the transfer of property, land, or real estate lacked location and date information.[131] This was changed when it was discovered that this could give rise to fraud.

It is also difficult to date the existing and surviving construction plans from the Middle Ages, because they do not contain dates, years, or the names of the respective draftsmen. It is therefore not uncommon for experts' opinions on the dating of a drawing to diverge widely in time (cf. section 3.2).

The problem of dealing with time in the Middle Ages is well illustrated by clocks. Mechanical clocks first appeared in the late 13th century, between 1277 and 1300.[132] At the beginning, there were only a few public clocks. They were located in churches, and had – surprisingly today – only one hand, the hour hand. The minute hand required more precise measurement than was possible at the time, and was not introduced until 1680.

With the introduction of clocks, which soon began to strike the hours from church and town towers, people's sense of time slowly began to change. People increasingly perceived time as something "objective" that ran independently of their lives and lifetimes, rather than simply orienting themselves to the position of the sun each day and living in the here and now. The perception of time changed over several centuries.

It is reported that even in the 16th century Martin Luther would not have known his date of birth when asked. People simply did not care where something happened in the past or when they were born. In the course of the process of European culture's becoming more literate, the measurement of time and space and the location of the individual in the objective space-time structure (independent of the subject) became increasingly important. This fact had an influence on construction plans that should not be underestimated.

Because the people in oral and preliterate cultures live "subjectively" in the here and now, thinking neither of the past nor of the future, a text written in a time other than their own is a mystery to them. In the early days of European literate culture, words like Villard de Honnecourt's introduction served as "bridging aids" to make comprehensible the unfamiliar new fact of the temporal-spatial separation of text / reader and author.

If people on the epochal threshold between preliterate and literate culture in the Middle Ages did not perceive time as something existing objectively and independently of them, this would also have an influence on their attitude towards construction plans and their realization. Certainly, neither master builders nor builder-owners thought about the need to make a precise construction plan, because it would be important in the future for later builders of the same building or for later repairs.

In the Romanesque period, and to some extent still in the Gothic period, this can be seen in recognizable changes during the building process itself, nowadays often interpreted as a "change of plan": When a new master builder arrived, he often continued to erect the cathedral in a different way than his predecessor. The people lived in "the here and now", without thinking about future master builders or later repairs of a building. According to Dieter Kimpel, there are

> *"structures in which such misunderstandings between successive architects accumulate in a significant way."*[133]

Was it really always a case of misunderstanding? Or was it rather intentional when a building was continued in a different form?

Was Villard's album an instructional book?

Let us return to Villard. The linguistic analysis of his choice of words as well as his remarks on geometry free us from viewing, evaluating, and understanding his work from the point of view of our contemporary literate culture – a culture that developed with the Renaissance. We can now better place Villard's work in the "zeitgeist of the Middle Ages".

Villard was certainly highly talented in drawing, as well as in construction and engineering. In this respect, he was an early pioneer of architecture. In addition, he developed or documented remarkable machines such as the sawmill.[134] He depicted them – typical of his time and also of the centuries that followed – in combined top and side views, i. e. in an ambiguous perspective. His three-dimensional drawings give an aid to perspective drawing by means of the lines applied to the plates.

Villard may have known Latin and been able to read like other authors of his time; he may even have read Euclid's "Elements" (*Stoicheia*) or other works on geometry and mathematics in a Latin translation at the advanced

Cistercian monastery of Vaucelles. The Cistercians were early pioneers of technical innovations from the 12th century onwards, and he may have already benefited from their know-how. The fact that he may nevertheless not have been able to write is not an argument against this, as it is typical for book authors between the 10th and the 15th centuries.

Vaguely and several centuries ahead of his time, Villard may already have had in mind the training as an architect or engineer by means of instructional books, such as his, with a "standardized canon of knowledge" including construction drawings, as his use of the word *enseigner* (English "to teach") expresses. He strove for this in words and pictures, and his Sketchbook shows, historically, the first beginnings of what this might look like. His statement, used several times, with the meaningful statement *"This is called geometry"* clearly points in this direction. However, on the threshold from the preliterate to the literate culture in the early 13th century, we may not expect a "perfect" textbook according to the modern state of our literate, knowledge- and education-based culture.

2.5 Islamic architecture – how Arab countries built without plans

The failed dialogue

We have noticed that we, as members of the present-day literate culture, are inclined to assume that the preliterate architects of the Middle Ages were capable of many things that they were indeed not, because they basically thought differently and proceeded differently in the planning of buildings than we do today. Unfortunately, we cannot verify this – we cannot consult a master builder of the Middle Ages to find out how he constructed a building, with or without written plans.

Miraculously, however, a dialogue between two construction experts from the Arab culture has come down to us shedding light on the matter: One of the two, named Ustad, is still completely entrenched in the oral culture; he can neither write nor read and worked as a master builder on a mosque in Isfahan. He likely acquired expertise in construction and related skills through hands-on experience and direct instruction from his father. The other one is literate and familiar with the principles of drawing because of his professional training. The literate participant in the dialogue is Arthur Upham Pope (1881 – 1969), a renowned U.S. expert on Iranian art, professor of philosophy and aesthetics, archaeologist, photographer, and museum director. In the 1920s, he was involved in the restoration and revival of Persian architecture, among other things, and was authorized by Shah Reza Khan Pavlavi to study the architecture of mosques and take photographs of them.[135]

The following dialogue took place between the two, in the early 20th century, probably in the 1920s. It is quoted by the Islamic scholar Jonathan M. Bloom:

> *"Then [Arthur Upham] Pope asked Ustad [a master mason from Isfahan] details of building a brick squinch. He seemed stumped. So I handed him a sheet of paper and a pencil. He held them at arm's length, a look of total hopelessness on his [...] face [...] He was illerate: more, he was incapable of presenting a three-dimensional object in two flat dimensions. He put the pencil aside, then folded the paper intricately to construct an actual squinch."*[136]

This shows how the master builder, shaped by an oral culture, cannot understand the literate expert in architecture at all. He cannot explain how he builds a round arch, typical for mosques, because he has practical experience, but lacks theoretical knowledge. "Nevertheless" he can build and construct these arches perfectly, even if he does not work with written plans. In other words, the motorist wonders about the rider who cannot explain to him how he moves. Unfamiliar items like "wheels, engine and steering wheel" make it difficult for the rider to describe their purpose and function since he lacks knowledge of them.

Incidentally, the fact that an architect in the Arab world of the early 20th century was illiterate was probably not an exception and may still occur today. The Arab countries have not become thoroughly literate to this day and in some cases remain true to their millennia-old preliterate culture. (To explain the reasons for this would go too far. In short, the persistence of the oral culture in the Muslim world probably has to do with the fact that the Arab states massively resisted the introduction of letterpress printing from the 14th century onward for religious reasons, so that books continued to be reproduced only by hand and thus in very small quantities. Printing presses were not introduced until the 19th century under massive European influence). According to Butschek[137], in 2000, 33 % of the Algerian, 29 % of the Tunisian, and 51 % of the Moroccan population were illiterate. As a travel guide in 2017 pointed out, Morocco still has an illiteracy rate of 30 to 40 %. These people are not on the margins of society, as is often the case with illiterates in Europe, but are integrated into the professional and economic life of their home countries. You will find an overview of the literacy rates of all countries in the world on the Internet.[138] The highest rates are found in Africa and Asia, especially in Muslim countries.

Let us note: The dialogue between the two experts in Islamic architecture failed. They could not communicate with each other and talked past each other, even though they both spoke Arabic. This gives us an idea that it is very difficult for us to understand, with the means of our present architecture and engineering, how the master builders of the Middle Ages conceived and constructed buildings and technical devices (running wheels, pedal cranes, fortifications, etc.). Our present principles as "thinking and calculating constructs" are, seen through the eyes of a medieval master builder, abstract, theoretical and at least partially incomprehensible.

In the 19th century, the well-known writer Victor Hugo considered the replacement of the Gothic by the Renaissance to be the *"death of architecture"*.[139] He must have felt that the "technical planning" of buildings, which had become increasingly consistent since the Renaissance and was no longer focused on the building process itself, had acquired something "soulless, mechanized, cold" – an impression that, from today's perspective, we perhaps attribute less to the Renaissance than to the buildings of the 20th and early 21st centuries. After the introduction of literate thinking, planning changed as well as the character of the buildings themselves.

If an architect, engineer, or structural engineer of today were to meet a master builder of the Middle Ages, the communication would probably be very similar to the example quoted: The medieval master builder could show directly on the object itself how he was going to proceed or what the final result would look like,

but he could not abstract from his practice of action to higher, general principles of geometry, of calculation, of the projection of a three-dimensional structure onto a two-dimensional surface, or of statics. He has what we call "intuitive" knowledge of action or experience.

Building by remembering and by copying

Islamic scholars face the same problem as architectural and art historians in Europe: there is a large number of early epochal buildings in Arab countries, some of which still exist today, for which design plans have never been found. Architectural drawings also appear in the Islamic world at the earliest in the 13th century and are not generally used until the 15th century.[140]

In Arab culture, as in Europe, there were early theoretical works on mathematics, e. g., by the famous Al-Chwarizmi (c. 780 – 835), who influenced both Arab and European culture. Al-Chwarizmi introduced, among other things, the Indian numbers and the zero, developed geometric solutions to linear and quadratic equations, and made astronomical calendar calculations.

Due to the pronounced mathematical know-how of the Muslim world, some Islamic scholars, such as Renata Holod, assume – analogous to European architectural and art historians – that the Arab builders must have had mathematical knowledge and would have put construction plans on paper, but they were lost.

As an Arabist, Jonathan M. Bloom – professor of Islamic culture and art in the U.S., to whom we owe the transmission of the enlightening dialogue between the two building experts – has not only dealt with the spread of paper in the Arab world in his standard work "Paper before Print" (2001), but also intensively with Islamic architecture.[141] He compiles source material and examines the whole thing from different angles. In doing so, he comes to the following conclusions: In the first five centuries of Islam (c. 622 – 1122), there were no architectural drawings at all.[142] Builders learned from other builders and used their memory as well as *"gestures"* to preserve and transmit plans and designs. In addition, they helped themselves in the following ways:

- They repeatedly used the hypostyle type of structure (resting on columns) for the buildings, with the first element – no matter whether it was a column, arch or vault – serving as a complete scale for the construction of all subsequent elements.
- They solved possible static problems by "overbuilding", i. e. they built walls, columns etc. stronger than necessary according to modern static criteria in order to avoid possible collapses.[143] This is also partly the case in Europe during the Romanesque period.
- The builders used other buildings as models and copied them. In North Africa, for example, the Great Mosque of Kairouan in Tunisia served as a model for later mosques in the region in the early 9th century. The tower of this mosque, in turn, was based in shape on a lighthouse built by the Romans centuries earlier and still standing near Salakta. Experts claim that the tower built by the Arabs was more cumbersome and monumental than its Roman counterpart. Here, as in Europe, we see that the construction knowledge available in antiquity was lost in subsequent centuries. Another important Islamic model was the Great Mosque of Damascus, which was copied, too, throughout the Arab world for centuries.[144]

A closer look at some buildings reveals that many things appear to be exactly right-angled to the eye of the beholder, but in reality they are not, as in the case of the mosque in Tunis, for example, where not a single right angle is exactly 90 degrees.[145]

The earliest surviving architectural plan from Islamic lands comes from the ruins of Takht-i Sulayman, the summer capital of the Mongols in the 13th century (in present-day Iran). It seems to have served to construct the typical Islamic stalactite ceiling vaults, the so-called *muqarnas*, from prefabricated plaster elements.[146] Here again, we see a parallel to European architecture: the surviving plans refer to building details, but not to the overall structure.

Beginning in the second half of the 14th century, plans were made in Tabriz, probably on paper, for the construction of the Rukn-al-Din tomb complex, including a madrasa ("Quranic school"), a hostel, a hospice for Sufis, a bazaar and a bath. Finally, the Topkapi scrolls on paper date from the 15th century. They were used to make architectural decorations – again, detailed drawings – and are still kept in the Topkapi Palace Library. In the same century, gridline paper also appears for the first time in plans in Tashkent (now Uzbekistan).[147]

Bloom points out an aspect that has not been addressed in the European discussion of the lost blueprints: Architectural drawings presuppose *a common visual notational system* (a codification) that allows a sender to encode messages in an unambiguous way and the receiver to decode them in turn. The architect as "sender" encodes his "message", namely how the building to be constructed should look like, in a drawing, and those working on the construction as "receivers" decode it in order to realize the plan.

Such a system of notation is necessary to bridge the difference between the idea of what three-dimensional space should look like and its two-dimensional conception in the form of plans, sections, and elevations. However, according to Bloom, a system of notation does not appear in the Arab world until around 1250, probably earlier in the eastern and later in the western countries of Islam.

The dissemination of a notation system is in turn tied to the availability of writing materials such as paper, which was available in Islam from the 9th/10th century onward, but was very expensive for a long time, since there was no mass production process in the Arab countries (as there was in Europe starting in the late 13th century). In the 10th century, for example, 125 sheets of paper cost as much as three months' income for a person in the lower middle class – I.e. about 4,500 euros in today's purchasing power in Europe.[148] That is, one sheet of paper cost the equivalent of about 36 euros. A standard pack of copying paper, for which we pay an average of around 4 euros today, would cost 18,000 euros according to the prices of the 10th century.

From his findings, Bloom concludes:

> *"In the realm of architecture, the increased availability of paper would have encouraged the use of personal notation for sketches and plans; the ease with which paper could be sent from one place to another would have fostered the development of collective systems of notation and the transfer of visual images over long distances. [...] Our reliance on notational systems has largely obviated the need for [...] mental feats and ensured similar, if not identical, performances over a wide space and long time, practices that our society values highly. [...] Finally, the emergence and use of notational systems brought about a further professionalization of architecture, for the ability to draw and read plans is a learned and complex skill, quite different in form that required to make buildings stand up."* [149]

In my opinion, Bloom correctly links the availability of writing materials and the development of a collective – or rather codified – notation system for construction plans. It applies equally to Europe (cf. section 4.4).

3. Sketching, scratching, and showing – plans on hard and soft materials

3.1 The cultural and economic boom of the 12th and 13th centuries

Many innovations lead to a cultural flowering

The 12th and 13th centuries, when the Gothic period developed, were a time of extraordinary economic as well as cultural growth in Europe. The strong increase of written documents can certainly be seen in this context. Some authors even speak of the "Renaissance" or the "commercial revolution of the Middle Ages".

The European population grew the most after new agricultural techniques – such as the introduction of the plow and the three-field farming – led to an abundance of food production in the early Middle Ages. Additionally, the introduction of the cummet harness and the horseshoe had the effect that heavy loads including stones for church building were now pulled by horses instead of oxen. The more agile horses allowed for faster transportation. Farmers were able to live further away from their fields due to the use of horses, so that larger villages rather than small, scattered settlements developed.

Various other technical inventions had the effect of simplifying work processes and thus serving manpower. This included the expansion of the milling industry. Mills were used not only to grind grain, but also to mill or felt fabrics.

In the construction sector, the introduction of the wheelbarrow and the tread wheel crane had a positive effect. The wheelbarrow replaced the second man on the stretcher, and the crane, driven by several henchmen or winchmen, by running in the treadle drum – as a mechanical elevator – enabled heavy loads to be lifted by simple means.

Figure 10: Drawing from the Maciejowski Bible or Crusader Bible, c. 1245 (Pierpont Morgan Library, New York, Ms M. 638, fol. 3r).
A construction site in the Middle Ages – a typical illustration: various details and activities of building operations are depicted: Tread wheel crane as elevator, stones, mortar, mortar trowel, stonemason's tools, transportation and processing of stones. But nowhere can be found a plan on parchment. This shows that it did not exist or was of no importance. It is probably the master builder who is checking the squareness of a hewn stone by using a protractor in the lower right of the picture. The picture is drawn on basis of aspective views (that means: without correct perspective, cf. section 4.3): Front and side views are mixed, clearly recognizable by the ladder that seems to float in front of the building.

Further remarkable inventions, whose origins and diffusion in history cannot always be precisely, contributed to the general upswing, such as the introduction of the nautical compass, the spinning wheel, and the weight-wheel clocks around 1270 to 1290. These clocks, which were reasonably accurate and independent of the position of the sun, introduced for the first time a new time consisting of "equally long" hours, making people independent of the position of the sun and the inaccurate sundials and water clocks.

The growth of the better-fed population, in turn, contributed to the fact that the cities experienced a greater influx than in the centuries before, especially in the west and south of Germany. An increasing number of cities acquired the privilege of being "free imperial cities", meaning that they were not directly subject to any territorial ruler, but only to the emperor. Citizen self-administration and self-governance began to emerge. This was the case, for example, with Strasbourg. When Strasbourg became one of the first free imperial cities of the Holy Roman Empire in 1262, the Notre-Dame workshop (Bauhütte) also came under the jurisdiction of the city. Henceforth, the church was no longer responsible for the erection of the cathedral, but the self-governing citizens.

The growth of cities caused a differentiation of crafts, because within the city walls society became more and more specialized in labor. Craftsmen had the opportunity to advance through technical specialization. Carpenters, for example, could become millwrights or master builders, blacksmiths could become armorers, toolmakers, farriers, and so on.[150] The architectural profession, as we shall see, also benefited from the onset of specialization, as did the art of building itself.

With the growth of the cities and the increasing productivity, long-distance trade also grew rapidly, and the number of merchants rose. As a result, the population was increasingly exposed to goods from the Orient, most of which found their way to Europe via Venice or the Iberian Peninsula. The city became an exchange of goods and knowledge.

The first universities were founded in Bologna (around 1088), Oxford (around 1095), Cambridge (1209), Paris (1253) and Montpellier (1289). Some of them developed from cathedral schools. This also broke new ground in education. New knowledge arose from the emerging scholarship, not least through contact with Arabic science.

Here, we recognize a "*whole complex of mutually complementary and reinforcing innovations*".[151] In the 12th and 13th centuries they led to a cultural and economic flourishing for which no single innovation or cause can be held responsible.

The emergence of the first construction plans around 1250

During this period of cultural prosperity, not only did the Gothic style reach its peak, but the first drawings on parchment also appeared. However, these were not constuction plans in the modern sense, which would have completely depicted entire buildings and thus provided a complete basis for planning. Rather, to use Walter Ong's metaphor, they corresponded more to the "horse" than to the "car", requiring much slower movement. The term "planning aid" would be appropriate for the early plans, which were elevations of the facade, not floor plans or cross-sections.

The earliest surviving plans from the Middle Ages – apart from the plan of the St. Gall monastery (cf. Figure 1) dating from around 825 – are the so-called Reims palimpsests, plans of Cologne Cathedral (cf. Figure 14) and Strasbourg Cathedral (cf. Figure 11, Figure 15).

The Reims palimpsests are facade sketches applied to a total of 153 sheets of parchment (used several times), of poor, namely rough, quality.[152] They were by no means used to plan and execute a specific building 1:1. Rather, they are drawings that were partially applied to the Abbey of St. Nicaise of Reims, partly for the cathedrals of Soissons and Amiens, and partly for no building at all.[153] Some drawings are exactly rectilinear, but sometimes contain drawing errors when identical columns vary in size; they were drawn entirely or partially freehand.

The art historian Robert Branner, who studied the Reims palimpsests in detail, concluded that they had been a kind of *"shorthand"* for reproducing spatial or structural concepts; they might also have been *"apprentice exercises"*. I would put it this way according to Branner's findings:

The Reims palimpsests were *artistic drafts* that did not have to be binding at all, but were allowed to have the character of sketches – very much like artists sketch a picture before bringing it to a "final" form. By no means all sketches are fully realized, sometimes only parts of them are incorporated into a picture, some are modified, and sometimes it remains with a sketch without its realization. In the same way that artists sketch pictures, builders sketched parts of buildings.

Why do elevation drawings suddenly appear around 1250, while for the centuries before that, for the Romanesque period or the early Middle Ages, no drawings exist, at least no evidence has been found until today?

Branner believes that the drawings were necessitated by structural changes in the High Gothic phase between 1230 and 1350. The Rayonnant style emerging in that period, with its maximally large window surfaces and rose windows, as well as the resulting savings in stone as a material, would have made it necessary to prepare project drawings of the facades in advance.[154] In other words, the drawings were not used to design a complete building, but attempts were made to develop individual parts in advance. They were to be realized in an unprecedented, innovative form. With the

Rayonnant style, the Gothic style completely emancipated itself from the Romanesque style, whose masonry construction used a lot of material for thick stone walls and knew only small windows.

In the 12th and 13th centuries, construction productivity increased significantly. People began to erect more buildings and to build faster than in the centuries before. In general, the causes are certainly to be found in the cultural and economic upswing of the time.

According to Dieter Kimpel, the stacking technique was used in order to speed up construction. Individual stone blocks – now also larger than before – were prefabricated, especially in winter, when work on the building had to be stopped due to rain and frost. The prefabrication of stones served to eliminate the winter unemployment of the stonemasons, who could now work in closed and heated rooms; this was also the origin to the stonemasons' lodges (Bauhütten).[155]

Then, in the following spring and summer the stone blocks produced in winter could be assembled in layers of the same height, saving a great deal of time. In some ways, the process is similar to what we know today as prefabricated construction, which has perfected the principle of industrial prefabrication of components followed by rapid assembly to form a building. However, in the Middle Ages, one cannot assume such strong standardization as is common today.

The prefabrication of building elements required more precise planning of the shape of the structure, as Kimpel said. The individual elements had to be precisely coordinated with each other so that the backfilling and assembly process could be carried out quickly during the frost- and rain-free period and so that no waste was produced during prefabrication. In addition, a more precise coordination was required between the quarry, the workshop and the construction site. For this reason, Kimpel says, architectural drawings were an indispensable planning tool.

However, architectural historians also argue the opposite. Building with the help of prefabricated elements, they argue, made construction plans superfluous because of their standardization.[156] The architect Stefan Amt is of the opinion that in the Gothic period the graphic representation of designs was unnecessary because of the *"extensive fixation of the spatial composition and the proportioning by fixed conventions."* [157] He adopted this view from Robert Oertel.[158] But building conventions have existed at all times, and they still exist today, nonetheless building plans have not been dispensed since the Renaissance.

The new construction method of stacking – including the prefabrication of building components with significantly larger stone blocks than in older church buildings – was probably first realized around 1200 in Soissons, around 1212 in Reims and around 1220 in the cathedral of Amiens.[159] The beginning of "standardization" is possibly related to the fact that, in the course of the economic boom in the 13th century and the associated upswing in coinage,[160] wages on construction sites were paid in money rather than in kind (natural products). This led to greater freedom in the labor market, but possibly also to an increase in labor costs. The goal was to counteract this. After all, standardized production or prefabrication always increases the speed of work – not only in the construction industry, but in general and even today – and thus reduces costs.[161]

However, the standardization may also be related to the fact that the wealth of experience of the master builders and craftsmen grew with each new Gothic church. Thus, in the High Gothic period (Decorated Style), it was already possible to access a body of knowledge that was not yet known in the Early Gothic period, when more experimentation was required. Standardizations or simplifications were created for building elements that had been used repeatedly and had proven to be optimal in a certain form.

No precise cause can be determined for the emergence of the first construction plans fixed on parchment in the middle of the 13th century. Some things, such as the desire for "standardization" or prefabrication in the building industry, may speak as much against the need for plans as for them. It is as if something new has emerged in the spirit of the times, and has begun to awaken simultaneously in many areas of society. In any case, the emergence of parchment plans fits into the overall cultural-historical impression of Europe at that time, which was characterized by an innovative awakening. With regard to the written form of the plans, it seems as if master builders followed the zeitgeist of the leaps and bounds of writing in Europe and now created sketches on parchment for the first time.

Dating the early construction drawings

Historians do not unanimously agree on the dating of the early drawings. In addition to those of Reims, they also include those of Cologne, Strasbourg, Vienna and some other cathedrals. Since the plans found do not include dates until about the 15th century, experts' estimates sometimes differ by 20 to 100 years. Barbara Schock-Werner, former master builder of the Cologne Cathedral, puts the Reims palimpsests as early as 1220, while Branner puts them around 1240/60.[162]

There is also a debate among experts, for example, about the drawings of Cologne Cathedral. While Marc Steinmann, after a thorough examination, dates them between 1277 and 1280, Johann Josef Böker places them around 80 years later, between 1350 and 1370.[163]

The *Notre-Dame Work Foundation of Strasbourg* (in French: *Fondation de l'Oeuvre Notre-Dame de Strasbourg*, in German: *Frauenwerk)* is one of the oldest Franco-German workshops (Bauhütten) to have existed continuously since around 1202. Due to its unique know-how, it has been declared a UNESCO Intangible World Heritage Site. The property of the foundation includes a number of parchment plans that are among the oldest in Europe, including the so-called "Plan A", dated to 1250/60 by the *Notre-Dame Work Foundation* itself.[164] Other plans were likely created between 1260/70 and 1510/15. All the plans that have survived up to 1494 are drawn on parchment, only the most recent plan from 1510/15 was drawn on paper.

Based on the dating of the economic and cultural flowering and achievements of this period, the first important drawings (Reims, Strasbourg, Cologne) can be dated with some certainty to the second half of the 13th century – around 1250/60 – but certainly not earlier.

Figure 11: The so-called "Plan A" of the Strasbourg Cathedral, made around 1250/60 (on parchment, 86 x 61 cm = 33,85 x 24 in), is the oldest architectural drawing in Strasbourg and one of the oldest surviving in Europe. It is in the possession of the *Notre-Dame Work Foundation of Strasbourg*.
The drawing shows a draft for the Gothic redesign of the lower southern part of the west facade, which was still Romanesque at the time and remained so until about 1275. The plan was probably made as a first draft before the facade was renewed in the Gothic style, but like so many other drawings it was not realized.

Changes in the profession – the first "star architects"

With the advent of building plans, the profession of architect also seems to have slowly changed. From about 1260, there is evidence that the master builder no longer worked on the construction site, at least not continuously. This is the time when the first "star architects" became known by name, while the master builders of earlier times remained unknown. The earliest architect known by name is William of Sens (c. 1110 – 80), a Frenchman who was the first to bring the Gothic style to England. He was the architect of Canterbury Cathedral. William was forced to stop work in 1180 as a result of a serious accident on the construction site and died shortly thereafter[165], before the cathedral was completed. For the early outstanding masters, one erected:

- tomb slabs as for Hugues de Libergier (c. 1229 – 63), the first architect of St. Nicaise in Reims (cf. Figure 12), and
- sculptures on or in churches as for Erwin von Steinbach (1244 – 1318), the first known architect of the Strasbourg Cathedral (cf. Figure 13).
- The masters were depicted in church mazes, as in the Cathedral of Amiens, or
- inscriptions were dedicated to them, as for Jean de Chelles (1200 – 60) on a pedestal in the south transept of *Notre Dame de Paris.*[166]

During this period, master builders experienced a rise in social status compared to craftsmen, enabling them to purchase land and houses.

Figure 12: Tomb slab of Hugues Libergier, the initial builder of St. Nicaise in Reims, from *Notre Dame de Reims* Cathedral, made in the late 13th century.

The architect is depicted as an elegant gentleman, holding the model of his church, measuring rod, protractor and compass (circled at the bottom right). The art historian Otto Kletzl interprets the compass as a proportional divider, while I perceive it as an elegant pressure compass that can be operated by one hand. The curved design, resembling a pair of pliers, makes it particularly convenient to use (cf. section 4.2).

Figure 13: Erwin von Steinbach (1244 – 1318), the first architect of the Strasbourg Cathedral to be identified by name, from 1277/84 – 1318, a 19th century sculpture on the south portal of the Cathedral.

Although the sculptor placed a plan in Erwin's right hand, no construction plans have survived from him. According to the *Notre-Dame Work Foundation,* the well-known "Plan A" (cf. *Figure 11*) was not drawn by Erwin, but by another draftsman, possibly his predecessor, whose name is uncertain.

In 1261, the Franciscan friar Nicolas Byard blasphemed that builders gave instructions to craftsmen but did not work themselves and yet received a higher wage. In the same way, but not blasphemously, but rather as a matter of course, Thomas Aquinas expressed in 1269 in his *Questiones de duodecim quodlibet* ("Twelve Questions on Various Subjects") that a master builder

> *"who carries out instructions concerning the building, although he does not work with his hands, hires himself out for a higher wage than the craftsmen who hew wood and cut stones."*[167]

The first master builder who is known to have been allowed to supervise two construction sites at the same time – namely in the cities of Evreux and Meaux, some 150 kilometers (= 93 miles) apart – was Gautier de Varinfroy. His contract with the cathedral chapter of Meaux dates from 1253.[168] The builders were supported by building administrators who managed the construction financially and organizationally.[169]

Barbara Schock-Werner asserts that after the emergence of the Reims palimpsests around 1220, the drawing *"very quickly developed into a mature and multifaceted carrier of ideas"*. This should have had the effect that the architect no longer had to be present on the construction site, but could *"plan in the office"*.[170] However, the development from the first drawings in Reims to mature building design plans did not happen "quickly" at all, but took until the 18th century, as I will show in the following chapters. It was not until the 15th/16th century that the art of planning had developed to such an extent that master builders were largely dispensable on the construction site.

In the 13th century and for a long time thereafter, plans were only made for parts of buildings on portable writing materials, and these were by no means advanced enough to place construction entirely in the hands of the craftsmen. There may have been individual master builders of important churches who excelled at drawing, but the majority of architects at that time probably continued to work entirely without plans, especially when it came to secular buildings such as "simple" town houses. In Provins (Belgium) in 1284, for example, the lack of plans meant that architects still relied on a verbose description of the building concept:

"In the name of the Father and of the Son and of the Holy Spirit, Amen. This is the estimate of the Friars Minor of Provins. First, the monastery will be leveled to the ground. And the front gable and side will be the same size as before, except that the side wing will rest on round piers and on stone arches, which in turn will occupy the length of the former wing. And the course of the arches will have the height dictated by the distance necessary to connect them to the entablature supporting the roofwork of the nave; and on this side there will be as many arches as there are bays between two tie beams, as the length of the old wing requires, and these arches will be of the size required by the roofwork. At the gable, an abutment [buttress] will be attached to the arch abutment on the yard side, with an overhang of 6 feet and a block stone of 3 feet. The abutment shall be supported by a slope above the support device of the gable."[171]

The crisis of the 14th century

In the 14th century, some of the advances made during the high medieval blossom of the 12th and 13th centuries were temporarily lost again. This was mainly due to the great plague epidemics that swept through various regions of Europe in several waves, decimating the population by a third and triggering a prolonged economic crisis with famines due to a failing agricultural sector.[172] In addition, there was the Little Ice Age, which led to a worsening of the climate.

The Hundred Years' War between England and France (1337 – 1453) also contributed to the loss of earlier achievements and led to frequent interruptions in construction, including a decline in qualifications in the building business.[173] After the great "gap" torn by the 14th century, it was not until the 15th century that the achievements of the 13th century could be resumed. This largely marked the end of the Gothic era and the beginning of the Renaissance, in which remarkable progress was made over the Middle Ages, not only in terms of drawing techniques and building planning (cf. section 4.3).

3.2 The origin and the use of plans on parchment

The drawing of the west facade of Cologne Cathedral

The early evidence of construction drawings allows some conclusions about their origin and use. The plans were drawn on parchments that were glued or sewn together to form large surfaces and reached considerable sizes. For example, Strasbourg Riss B, dating from around 1260/70, is 2.75 m (= 9.02 ft) high and 70 cm (= 27.55 in) wide; another Strasbourg Riss (no. 5), striking for its unusual coloring (cf. Figure 15), dated to 1360/70 and attributed to Master Gerlach, is 4,05 m (= 13.28 ft) high and 86 cm (= 33.85 in) wide.[174]

Riss F of the Cologne Cathedral (cf. Figure 14), dated by Marc Steinmann to about 1280, consists of 20 individual parchments of very different sizes glued together, reaching a total height of impressive 4,06 m (= 13.32 ft) and a total width of 1,66 m (= 5.44 ft). The parchments vary in size. The size of the individual parchments varies from narrow strips of 4,2 x 8 cm (= 1.65 x 3,15 in) to dimensions of 80,5 x 77 cm (31.69 x 30.32 in).[175]

This suggests the need for a suitable writing material: The only way to create large drawing surfaces that allowed a sufficient resolution of the details to be depicted was only possible by "improvising", by gluing together whatever sheets of parchment were available, regardless of size and quality.

The question is whether the drawings were first applied to the individual parchment sheets and then glued together or vice versa. For the northern half of the Cologne drawing F it is documented that the parchments were first glued and then drawn.[176] But afterwards there were problems with the southern half of the same drawing, which was made separately from the northern part. This is because both halves had to be glued together as a whole after they had been completed in order to create an overall picture of the western facade.

This resulted in a shortcoming: there is a deviation of 1 cm (= 0.39 in) in the height of the drawn halves between the northern and southern parts. Experts have proven that this discrepancy is neither due to the uneven shrinkage of the parchment sheets nor to an incorrect gluing process, but to the fact that the northern and southern halves were drawn separately.

In fact, the two halves show different drawing qualities: The south side is much more sketchy and inaccurate, partly with recognizable construction problems. According to this, both halves were executed by different draftsmen[177], and "too many cooks spoiled the broth".

On additional drawings of the Cologne Cathedral, as well as on parchment drawings in general, it is evident that not only the overall plan could distort, but also certain individual parchment pieces of which it was comprised.[178]

All in all, early drawers faced challenges with using parchment as their writing medium: it was too small, could not be obtained in one piece in modern sizes, sometimes had to be sewn or glued together from many individual pieces, and warped even at low humidity. Each sheet of a parchment could stretch or contract differently. Even the best drawing technique is useless if no suitable writing medium is available! It had to be planned differently. The many surviving drawings of building details on wood, plaster, or stone convey a clear message: even though it was difficult to

carve something into these hard materials, it was imperative as it prevented any risk of distortion or using incorrect measurements as a basis.

Figure 14: Drawing F of the Cologne Cathedral, produced around 1280, shows the design of the west facade. In the original it was 4,06 meters high (= 13.32 ft) and 1,66 meters (= 5.44 ft) wide, consisting of 20 parchments glued together. Presumably, all or a part of the drawing was made by Master Arnold, the second master builder of Cologne Cathedral.

Building plans as blueprints for many buildings

In some respects, the Cologne plans are atypical. They were created by Master Arnold and were mostly built according to their original design, which sets them apart from the Reims palimpsests and the Strasbourg plans, as well as many other plans that have been discovered.[179]

The researchers have collected many parchment plans, which were often implemented

- in modified form, or only partially,
- or not at all,
- or even in completely different places, and sometimes even several times.
- Sometimes, they were partly realized much earlier than at the respective construction site and place where they were found, while in other cases, they were implemented 50 to 60 years later at the same site.

This shows that the Middle Ages had a completely different idea of the drawings and their purpose than we have of modern plans. As already explained, they served as sketches in the artistic sense, sometimes also as "blueprints" that were simply copied, since at that time there was no copyright to protect the individual work against copying. Unlike today, "design" was not considered worthy of protection, and copies were not considered plagiarism.

For example, the facade plan A designed for Strasbourg Cathedral (cf. Figure 11) was executed exclusively on the southwest portal of the cathedral of Freiburg im Breisgau (Germany). And the main window of the Cologne cathedral

Figure 15: Detail from the plan 5 of the Strasbourg Cathedral, made around 1360/70 (on parchment, 4,05 x 0,86 m = 13.28 x 2.82 in), attributed to Master Gerlach.
The plan shows the central part of the west facade up to the level of the base of the spires, including the bell tower, rose window, and apostle gallery. Unusually for parchment drawings, it is partially colored in the upper area, suggesting that it was intended to impress clients with its aesthetics. The minster workshop *Notre-Dame Work Foundation of Strasbourg,* owner of the drawing, appraises it as "detailed but not exact" (cf. Fondation). The lower part of the design was executed, but the upper one was abandoned in favor of a wall connecting the north and south towers.

workshop was realized on the north transept of Altenberg (Germany) as well as on the west facade of St. Elisabeth in Marburg an der Lahn (Germany), at a time when its construction had not even begun in Cologne.[180] This indicates that the plan from Cologne circulated quickly among building experts. The "Visierung" (German term, mainly used in the Middle Ages and the Renaissance, for a drawing, design, outline drawing, blueprint, or sketch) of the sacrament house for St. George in Nördlingen, on the other hand, designed around 1470, was not executed until 1533 by another master at the same location.[181]

The Palatine Chapel in Aix-la-Chapelle (Germany) containing Charlemagne's tomb was reconstructed several times between the 9th and 12th centuries, in Compiegne (France), Hereford, Goslar and Ottmarsheim (Germany).[182] Sometimes plans were even brought from far away: When King Sigismund of Hungary wanted a hospital to be built in Buda in 1414, he sought copies of the *Ospedale della Scala* in Siena (Italy).[183]

We can conclude from this: Even in the case of important church buildings, originality or uniqueness in today's sense was not a concern. The blueprints made for a building must have circulated quickly and frequently between the construction workshops and the master builders, unless the master builders themselves took them with them on their way to the next construction site.

The early plans, unlike the modern drawings, were not exclusively for the purpose of planning and implementation of a very specific, new building, as the modern drawings do. As it seems, they fulfilled quite different functions:

- As presentational drawings, they were intended to convince builders (like the colored plan 5 of the Strasbourg Cathedral, cf. Figure 15).
- Individual building elements, especially the facades of planned buildings, were sketched, often in a non-binding way, but apparently more in an artistic manner.
- They were used as patterns and templates for very different buildings.

- They served as teaching and learning materials for the masters themselves, and certainly for the journeymen.
- They subsequently documented the construction of buildings already erected, some of them in the work of Villard de Honnecourt.
- They were used to collect donations as "show diagrams".[184]

Oversized drawings were sometimes publicly displayed in a central location to persuade people in one place to donate to a planned church. For this purpose, instead of large facade plans, "miraculous" relics were often sent on journeys, such as after the fire of Laôn Cathedral, when canons and lay people in northern France and even as far away as England went from place to place to collect donations.[185]

As it seems, the drawings were used manifold before they found their final and exclusive modern purpose: contractual character, design and execution of one – and only one – very specific building.

Pattern collections and plan treasures

Parchment drawings were collected in the stonemasons' workshops (Bauhütten) and by the master builders themselves. They were valuable and, in an age before printed books and systematic training, they served as a collection of "samples" that could be used at will and without legal consequences. They helped to expand the spectrum of knowledge[186] as well as to facilitate one's own design work. The two individually used sketchbooks by Villard de Honnecourt and Hans Hammer (cf. section 2.4) can also be understood as collections of patterns.

Collections of plans presuppose that a sufficient number of plans were already available and "in circulation" between the workshops (Bauhütten) and masters. If we assume that the first plans on parchment were produced around 1250/60, it took a little more than a century for the collections to reach a significant size. This point seems to have been reached by the end of the 14th century: The way plans had been handled before changed, and their importance grew. However, there were still no overall plans north of the Alps in a present-day sense recording a building as a whole and completely in advance.[187]

From the middle of the 15th century, new practices were introduced unknown in earlier centuries: The employment of master builders was made dependent on the submission of binding construction plans, as in the contract for Hans Puchsbaum at St. Stephen's in Vienna in 1446, in which the master builder also had to certify that he had borrowed older plans from the workshop.[188]

Compared to the 13th and 14th centuries, the importance of plans increased in the 15th century: The plan itself, rather than the finished building, became valuable and took on a legally binding character.

The collections of plans created by workshops (Bauhütten) and master builders were valuable objects. In principle, plans that a master builder drew on behalf of a client became the property of the respective workshop. However, the master builders also made collections of their own, as this made them independent of the workshop and enabled them to make supraregional comparisons. The sons of a master builder – often master builders themselves – sometimes received their father's drawing estate if they had proven themselves worthy according to the statutes of the lodge. This is what happened in Strasbourg in 1523, where the "arts locked in a chest" (German original: *künst in einem trog verschlossen)* were, in fact, secured with a shared key[189], only to be passed down to the sons once they had demonstrated their worthiness in subsequent years.

As the plans gained value, ownership disputes emerged: Niclas Queck, the chief master builder of Frankfurt Cathedral, was compelled to surrender one of his tower plans in 1503, six years after resigning, as he had unlawfully transported it to a construction site in Mayence.[190]

If drawings on parchment were carefully collected, stored and passed on, if they were regarded and treated as valuable objects, the assertion made by Conrad, Booz and Gimpel that many plans no longer needed were destroyed after their realization does not make sense either.[191] In fact, the opposite appears to be true: From about the 14th century onward, all the plans that could be obtained were guarded like treasures, copied and distributed in a controlled manner, their ownership legally regulated, and kept as teaching and illustrative material for masters and journeymen even after the completion of a building.

From the 15th century onward, the personal presence of a master builder became increasingly replacable by plans. However, in my opinion, this was only exceptionally possible during 12th and 13th centuries for a few "star architects" with highly developed drawing skills but was by no means the rule.

It also happened that master builders supervised a building exclusively by means of a plan, without ever visiting the construction site or even laying eyes on the building. In 1416, for example, Michael Savoy, who had been commissioned by St. Gall to design a tower, sent his son to the construction site with the finished plan.[192] Some master builders were also commissioned to design plans for individual structural elements of buildings that were otherwise overseen by other architects.

3.3 Stone, wood, and wax as plan support

Drawings and "Visierungen"

Terms like "blueprint" or "(architectural) drawing" are of modern origin. In the Middle Ages, the term "Visierung" was used in the German language, in Latin texts called as *designamentum*. The German word for architectural drawings, made with the help of compasses, "(Werk-)Riss", is related to the German words "ritzen" and "reißen" which are etymologically closely related to the English word "write". The original meaning of "write" as well as "ritzen" is "incise", "engrave" or "carve".[193] Historically, the term refers to carving a text or an image into a *hard* material, certainly not soft parchment or paper, but wood or stone. Carving on hard material required a high level of force, and sharp, hard metal instruments. In contrast, writing and drawing on parchment or paper was much easier; quills soaked in ink were all that was needed.

The German term "Visierung" is derived from the Latin word *videre* (meaning "to see"). In the Middle Ages, "Visierung" meant something like *"to model, depict or portray artfully."*[194] In its meaning of "modeling a building" the term is first documented in 1272 in connection with a shrine to be made at the monastery of Nivelles in Belgium.[195] In the building sector, "Visierung" became established as an expression for legally binding working drawings in the 15th century.[196]

But the term "Visierung" has still another meaning, namely "to set one's eyes on a target, to focus one's attention on something, to observe carefully, to aim". In relation to the use of the compass, this meaning is important because it gives a clue as to how the early construction drawings might have been made (cf. section 4.2).

Drawings encarved in stone

Besides parchment, other materials were used for planning, and these were wax, wood, stone and plaster. Incised drawings on stone are not an achievement of the European Middle Ages, but have also been handed down from earlier epochs and other cultures. On the stone roofs of the Egyptian temple of Edfu, for example, several damaged drawings were discovered, including a construction drawing of almost 2,50 m (= 8.2 ft) for the cornice of one of the two towers of the entrance area.[197]

According to Wolfgang Schöller, who has studied stone carvings of the European Middle Ages in detail, the first verifiable ones date from the period between 1190 and 1200, namely from England (Byland) and France (Chalons-sur-Marne).[198] Some of them were not carved directly into the stone, but on a layer of plaster previously applied to the stone; with the help of the plaster, a flat drawing surface was created.

Carved drawings on stone usually depicted certain building elements, often tracery and its design, in 1:1 scale, i. e. in their original size. Sometimes whole building sections were also carved into stone at a reduced scale in order to solve planning problems of the building construction in advance. In addition to the reproduction of building elements, there were also carvings of Archimedean spirals, which allowed the architect to determine the multiples of root 2 with the help of a straightedge.

According to Schöller, the stone carvings served two main purposes:

- the production of wooden templates, which – in contrast to the stone – allowed the exact cutting of the stone or plaster in question, and
- the subsequent control of whether a stone had been accurately cut by placing it on the stone carving and comparing its shape with that of the carving.[199]

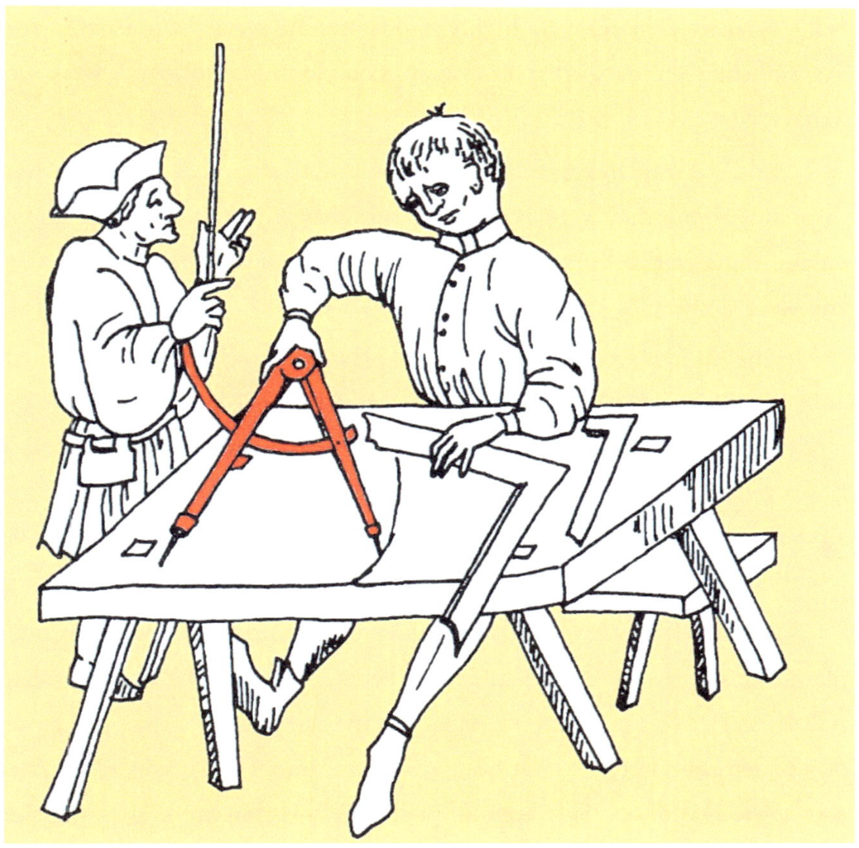

Figure 16: A master builder at a wooden, stone or plaster drawing board with a bow compass and a protractor. Depiction of a 15th-century Italian Euclid manuscript (here: black-and-white drawing based on the colored original: London, British Library, Add. Ms. 15692 f. 29v; compass colored red by the author).

Wooden templates

It was only a small step from stone carvings to wooden templates. It seems that the production of the two was closely related in terms of construction, although this is not proven. The communications researcher Lon R. Shelby believes that templates were highly important and were the *primary instruments* of the architects, whereas drawings on parchment or paper were secondary.[200]

Wooden templates have not survived due to the perishable nature of the material, but they were a common tool. They are said to have been hung on the walls of the workshops (Bauhütten) for constant use and control, and were sometimes made of lead instead of wood.[201]

In the Middle Ages, the wooden templates were referred to in German as "Maßpreter" ("dimensional boards"), "Modeln" or "Mödlen" ("models"); a modern term would be "profile gauge". From the late Middle Ages onward, it was the task of the foreman, the person who directed the construction of a building, to mark out the stones according to the dimension boards and to check them.

For more difficult pieces, the master builder made the wooden templates himself. This is documented for the late Middle Ages, e. g. for Heinrich III Parler of Ulm (c. 1391). As late as the 15th century, the production of wooden templates was considered so important that it was sometimes even entrusted to specially appointed and well paid masters, as in the case of the cathedral of Ulm in 1418.[202]

It can be concluded that planning in the 15th century (and beyond) consisted of a "mixed" use of stone or plaster carvings, wooden templates, and (parchment) drawings. Each medium performed *different* tasks in the course of construction, and none of them covered *all* functions. What was not covered by these media had to be "improvised," that is, decided and realized ad hoc during the ongoing construction process.

Apart from templates, wood was also used to represent scaled-down models of a planned building[203] – models that are still represented in plaster today. However, such "3D models" which are also said to have been made of wax seem to have been the exception in the Middle Ages. They have not been preserved.

Wax tablets, the "notepads" of the Middle Ages

In addition, wax tablets were probably used for planning in written form (cf. Figure 17). Although no wax tablets with architectural drawings have survived from the Middle Ages, there are written sources that indicate that sketches of floor plans were drawn on them. Gerbert of Aurillac (10th century) and a Cistercian monk (12th century) confirm their use in the Middle Ages.[204] There is evidence that small building sketches, descriptions or floor plans were "noted" on wax tablets from around 680 – and in some cases considerably earlier, namely in the ancient world.[205]

Wax tablets are wooden boards coated with wax that, in the absence of other writing materials, generally served as notepads or memo pads in ancient and medieval times. They were used by anyone who could read and write. There were single tablets and those that were bound together with wire or hemp to form a kind of "notebook"; the various sizes in which they have survived roughly correspond to today's European DIN-A7 (2.9 x 4.1 in) to DIN-A5 formats (5.8 x 8.3 in). A wax tablet was scratched with a pointed metal stylus, a fact that should not be forgotten. Later, the wax was smoothed out again with the help of the flattened side of the writing stylus to create a flat wax surface again for further inscription.[206]

While the mostly wooden wax tablets have not survived over the centuries, many metal writing styli have. Throughout Europe, archaeologists found such styli between Riga and Basel, on the one hand near former long-distance trade routes and on the other hand *"in close connection with important ecclesiastical buildings of the High Middle Ages"*[207], especially from the period between the 12th and 14th centuries.

Figure 17: Two wax tablets with writing stylus, bound together to form a "two-sided notebook", a so-called dyptichon. The back of the writing stylus is flattened to smooth out any scratching in the wax.

The unusual shape of some of the styli has led archaeologists to conclude that they may have come from Lombard builders in northern Italy, as they were often brought north across the Alps for building contracts since Charlemagne.[208] The unusual length and deformation of many styli also suggest that they were used not only for writing on wax tablets, but also for marking workpieces on stone.[209]

The small wax tablets were certainly not suitable for detailed and long-term construction planning or for precise, true-to-scale drawings that were to be preserved and passed down over several years or decades, but were merely reminders for the respective master builder or stonemason. Their contents were erased as soon as the note had served its purpose.

3.4 The drawing skills of medieval builders

How it was drawn on parchment

For decades, it was widely believed that the process of applying a drawing to parchment was as follows: With the help of blind groove pins (pointed metal pins), recessed construction lines were scratched into the parchment. After that, the blind grooves were traced with a drawing pen tempered with soot ink or iron gall ink.[210] The circles were drawn by using a compass to mark them as blind grooves in the parchment and then tracing them with ink.

In reality, however, a completely different approach was used. Modern digital examination methods allow the centuries-old plans to be enlarged by high resolution. Researchers no longer need to rely on the naked eye to reconstruct the drawing method, but can discover unknown details. Recent research has come to very different conclusions.

Dieter Büker used digital methods to systematically examine the earliest surviving plan of the Middle Ages, the St. Gall monastery plan (cf. Figure 1), and found the following: The circumference of circles and the course of straight lines were marked with small hairline stitches, so-called "pinpricks" (puncture points), but only at *single* points, by using an awl, a compass tip, or a graver. Subsequently, the circles or lines along the optical pinpricks as guide points were traced *freehand* – and accordingly inaccurately – with a stamped pen, sometimes from different positions.[211]

The same process of pricking and freehand tracing of "imaginary" lines marked only by *punctual* stitches, was also used in monastic scriptoria to mark the type area and the lines of writing on a sheet of parchment before inscribing it with a text.

In this way, not only the St. Gall monastery plan was created, but also other parchment building plans from the 13th century onwards. In 1958, Robert Branner first proposed that the Reims palimpsests were pricked. Subsequently, in 2011, Robert Bork confirmed this through empirical evidence on an expanded set of medieval plans. Büker also supported this finding through digital procedures.[212]

Blind grooves for circles or horizontal lines, on the other hand, cannot be determined from the plans; Büker refers to this as the *"hunt for a phantom"*.[213] Blind groove pins have not survived either, as Peter Pause noted in 1973.[214] Where apparently blind grooves are visible on the parchment, it is a deception of the eye based on the fact that the bird quill spread during the drawing process when the writing pressure was too strong. Thus, at times, two lines appear side by side like parallels on a parchment plan. One of them is the supposed blind groove – a deepening without ink – and the second one is the line drawn freehand using a reed pen tempered with ink. Errors, such as inaccurately drawn lines or letters, were corrected by scraping them off with an eraser knife – a common practice on parchment. Such knives can be seen in almost all medieval illustrations of scribes (cf. Figure 8). Exactly the same procedure was used to write books or documents. Ornaments or sculptural decoration were also drawn freehand with reed pen or goose quills.[215]

Recent research shows: Drawing compasses could not be used on parchment. Rather, all the drawings – circles as well as straight lines – were done freehand, with only individual points marked beforehand by small punctures (pinpricks). Presumably, the parchment skin, depending on its type and thickness, would have torn if too much pressure had been applied along a

longer blind groove line or circle. The resulting holes or larger longitudinal or transverse tears would have rendered it unusable. Blind grooves or blind circles would have had the effect of a knife cut, rendering the parchment unusable.

Therefore, one would have proceeded as carefully as possible, always limiting oneself to only a few punctual pinpricks in order to avoid major damage to the valuable writing material. This means:

1. If lines had to be drawn freehand on the parchment, this inevitably led to inaccuracy in drawing (and planning).
2. The compass had at most a subordinate (or no) function as a drawing tool for drafting on the writing material parchment.

Experts who have intensively studied various architectural drawings repeatedly emphasize their varying craftsmanship: some show glaring errors, others appear clumsy in certain areas, and still others are already decidedly professional for their respective times.[216] According to Völkle, this indicates that

> *"during an era that did not yet know standardized drawing, the personal talent and ability of the draftsman played a major role."* [217]

Projection techniques of the drawings

Experts who have intensively examined the early plans from the 13th and 14th centuries stress that they already show a – more or less correct – orthogonal projection[218], sometimes supplemented by incorrectly mapped drawing elements. That is to say, each "real" point on the drawing plane was mapped geometrically accurately so that the line connecting the points and their drawing images on the plane formed a right angle (orthogonal). Villard de Honnecourt also mastered orthogonal projection, as can be seen in his sketchbook (c. 1240).[219]

In itself, the orthogonal projection is nothing unusual; it is also documented in earlier cultures thousands of years ago, for example in Egypt for the drawing of a sphinx.[220] What is surprising, however, is the fact that it suddenly appeared on parchment plans in Europe in the 13th century, apparently without any predecessors or development, except for stone carvings and wooden templates.

The orthogonal projection as such, however, does not meet the requirements of planning in the modern sense of perspective, since some things are depicted in a spatially foreshortened way, as Peter Pause notes:

> *"By these means, an effect is achieved that approximates and emanates from the visual impression, not from the requirements of the building design".*[221]

Among the early drawings of the 13th and 14th centuries, the number of elevation drawings is outstanding. Often there are no floor plan drawings at all, and when there are, floor plans and elevations are often placed arbitrarily and combined on one sheet, but not based on a method that accurately aligns the two projections.[222] Projecting multiple sectional planes into a floor plan structure was a common procedure in the Gothic period, but one that made the implementation of the plan difficult because the exact position of the points in space could only be partially represented.

Even in the 12th century, it was considered almost impossible to develop the ground plan and the elevation plan in the same way and to the same scale – an indispensable condition for the overall planning of buildings from a "modern" point of view. Thus, Richard of St. Victor (c. 1110 –

73), an Augustinian and leading theologian of Paris, noted in his Ezekiel commentary that from a floor plan drawing one could

> *"easily extract place, location and number, texture, size, proportion. But since it is difficult or even impossible to reproduce length and width and height of buildings in the surface in one and the same drawing, I believe that it is sufficient if the location and place of all things [...] have been brought into the right form and the foundation of all these things has been laid, as it were, by proportionally drawn lines. For if we look at the lines, which are measured according to proportionate measurement, and understand by them nothing else than, as it were, the laid or designated foundations of the walls, it is at the same time easy to understand how the walls rise in height from this guidance of the lines and how on these walls the roof is laid".* [223]

In other words, if the floor plan is fixed, it is relatively easy to derive the elevation from it. In fact, this was probably done more often than the surviving drawings indicate.

The author of this book projected the floor plan and elevation of the *Notre Dame de Chartres Cathedral* (located 90 kilometers/56 miles southwest of Paris), a High Gothic church, one on top of the other to scale (cf. Figure 18). No drawings of this church have survived, and it is still not clear whether and how it was planned and built in detail. The superimposition reveals surprising correspondences up to the height of the towers of the west facade and the "congruence" of the position of the large rose window on the west facade and the maze on the floor of the cathedral.

In his extensive compilation of plans, the architectural historian Johann Josef Böker found floor plan drawings, some of which were drawn on the same scale and on the same sheet as the corresponding elevations. With growing productivity in building, which certainly led to an increase in learning, a more "complete" planning on parchment or paper slowly

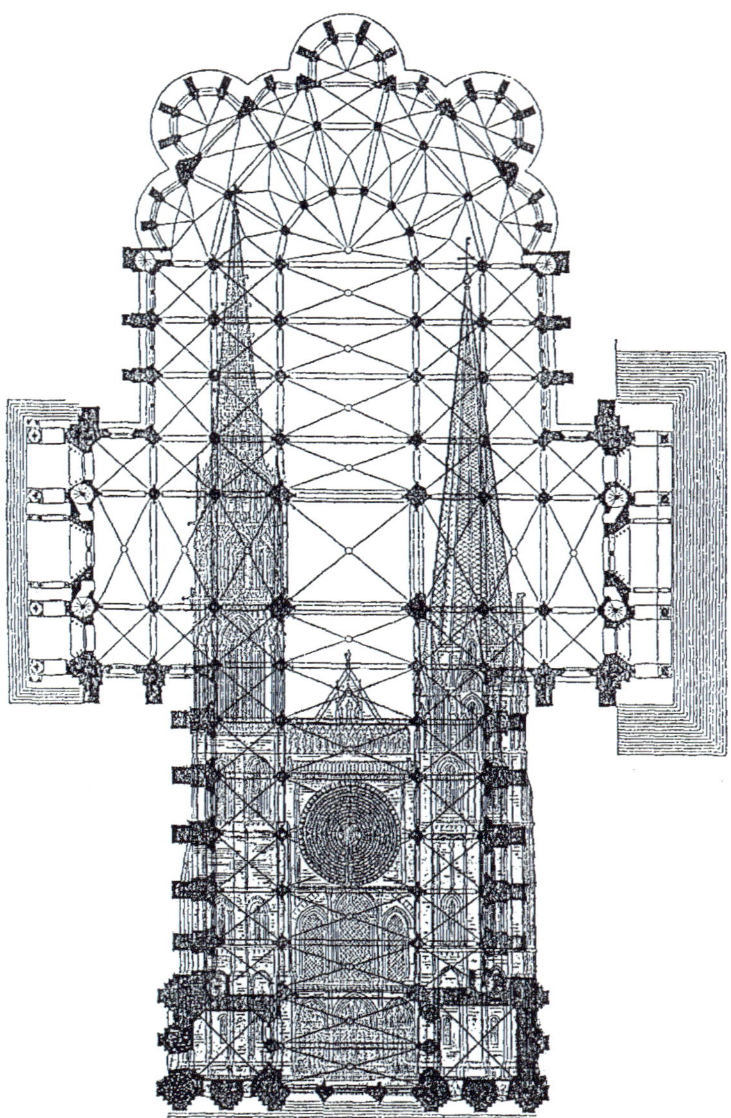

Figure 18: Projection of the ground plan and the elevation of *Notre Dame de Chartres Cathedral*, superimposed at the same scale. Exactly in the place where the maze is placed inside the cathedral, the large rose window of the west or main portal is placed in the elevation, even in the same size (projection of the author).

emerged, apparently beginning in the 14th century. In this new type of plan, the ground plan and the elevation were already related to each other.

Despite the display and drawing errors on the parchment plans, their drawing quality and their at least "largely maintained" perspective is astonishing when compared, for example, with the images of book illumination from the same period. These are not perspective at all, but aspective (cf. section 4.3).

Measures on the building ground instead of floor plan drawings on parchment

In both ancient and medieval times, drawings of floor plans were not documented on portable writing materials such as papyrus or parchment. Instead, the measurements were taken *directly on the construction site.*

There have been numerous misunderstandings and research errors regarding this fact, with the core of the issue traced back to a misinterpretation of a specific passage in an ancient manuscript, as uncovered by Günther Binding.

Marcus Vitruvius Pollio, a prominent Roman architect and engineer of the 1st century B. C., presented crucial insights of his time into the field of architecture and the skills of architects in his fundamental work *De architectura libri decem* ("Ten Books on Architecture"). His standard work on architecture was translated many times from Latin into various vernacular languages and was also known in the Middle Ages. Since the 8th century, it was copied again and again. In the 13th century, the interest in Vitruvius reached its peak when his book was systematically summarized by Vincent of Beauvais in the most important encyclopedia of the Middle Ages, the *Speculum Maius*, the "Great Mirror". The art of building was understood as *ars mechanica* ("mechanical art") and as an independent field of knowledge with many subfields.[224]

With the advent of letterpress printing, Vitruvius' work was also translated into German several times, first by Walther Hermann Ryff (Rivius) in 1548. From the 20th century, there are two German translations by Jakob Prestel (1912/14) and Curt Fensterbusch (1964). In both cases, especially one text passage from the 1st chapter of Book 1 was mistranslated. It concerns the following Latin passage that describes the relationship between architecture and geometry:

> *"Geometria autem plura praesidia praestat architecturae; et primum ex euthygrammis circini tradit usum, e quo maxime facilius aedificiorum in areis expediuntur descriptiones normarumque et librationum et linearum directiones."*

Curt Fensterbusch translates this in German in the following way (translated below from German into English):

> *"Geometry, however, offers several aids to architecture: namely, after the use of the ruler, it teaches the use of the compass. This will simplify in particular the drawing of buildings on the drawing board* [aedificiorum in areis descriptiones] *and the alignment of right angles, horizontal surfaces and straight lines."*
>
> (Original in German: *"Die Geometrie aber bietet der Architektur mehrere Hilfen: und zwar vermittelt sie zuerst nach dem Gebrauch des Lineals den Gebrauch des Zirkels, wodurch sie ganz besonders das Aufzeichnen von Gebäuden auf dem Zeichenbrett* [aedificiorum in areis descriptiones] *und das Ausrichten rechter Winkel, waagerechter Flächen und gerader Linien erleichtert."*)[225]

His translation follows that of Jakob Prestel, who renders the same sentence in the following way (again translated from German into English):

"Geometry (field metrology), on the other hand, provides the art of building with many practical aids, as it is primarily that the use of the ruler [euthygrammum – *ruler, straightedge] and the compass is taught by them. With the help of these instruments one can draw the plans* [descriptio – *plan drawing] of the buildings on the image frame* [area [....]], *as well as one can determine the layout of the angles* [norma [...]], *the horizontal surfaces together with the lines [...] surrounding the plan."*

(Original in German: *"Die Geometrie (Feldmesskunst) reicht hinwieder der Baukunst vielfache praktische Hilfsmittel dar, wie denn vornehmlich durch sie der Gebrauch des Lineals* [euthygrammum – *Lineal, Richtscheit] und des Zirkels gelehrt wird, mit deren Beihilfe man ohne besondere Geschicklichkeit die Pläne* [descriptio – *Planzeichnung] der Gebäude auf dem Bildrahmen* [area [...]] *aufzutragen, sowie die Anlage der Winkel* [norma [...]], *der waagerechten Flächen nebst der den Plan umgrenzenden Linien [...] zu bestimmen vermag.")* [226]

In essence, the two Latin terms *area* and *descriptio* have been mistranslated. Binding proves that *area* does not mean "drawing board" or "picture/image frame", but "building site, building area, construction area". In this sense, the term appears more often in Vitruvius and is also translated correctly several times in later text sections by Prestel and Fensterbusch. *Area* is frequently documented from the 6th to the 15th century in the sense of "building site", for example in texts by Isidore of Seville (560 – 636), Hrabanus Maurus (c. 780 – 856), Bishop Meinwerk in Paderborn (c. 975 – 1036) and last but not least in the work *De re aedificatoria* ("On Building") written by Leon Battista Alberti in 1450; but nowhere does *area* appear in the sense of "drawing board".[227]

Vitruvius' term *descriptio* is interpreted by Fensterbusch as "drawing", by Prestel as "plans" or "plan drawing", but in general it means "depiction, determination" or "arrangement". In this sense, the term can be found again by various authors from the 12th to the 15th century. "Drawing", "sketch", or "outline", on the other hand, is called *lineamentum* in Latin.[228] (I am sure that such mistranslations of Vitruvius from Latin can be found in languages other than German, too.)

Due to modern mistranslations, Vitruvius' "representations / arrangements on the building site" became "drawings on the drawing board" – certainly a misinterpretation caused by modern times. In the 20th century, the traditional method of laying out ground plans on the building site during antiquity and the Middle Ages became unimaginable with the introduction of building plans on the drawing board. There was a significant shift in building practices that occurred due to advancements in technology during this period. As Walter Ong metaphorically put it, the "horse" transitioned into the "secret car".

According to Binding, Vitruvius' text should be translated correctly in this manner (transferred from German to English below):

> *"Geometry, however, offers several aids to architecture; first of all, it conveys the use of the compass from straight lines [...]. Through this, the representations (or arrangements, determinations) of the buildings on the building sites* [aedificiorum in areis descriptiones] *and the alignments of the rectangular measures, the levelings, and the plumb lines are more easily prepared."*

> (Original in German: *"Die Geometria [= Feldmesskunst] aber bietet der Architektur mehrere Hilfen; und zwar vermittelt sie zuerst von geraden Linien aus [...] den Gebrauch des Zirkels, wodurch im höchsten Maß leichter die Darstellungen (oder Anordnungen, Bestimmungen) der Gebäude auf den Bauplätzen* [aedificiorum in areis descriptiones] *und die Ausrichtungen der*

> *Rechtewinkelmaße, der Nivellierungen und der Richtschnüre hergerichtet werden.")* [229]

The mistranslations also led to Vitruvius' term *ichnographia* being interpreted as "ground plan (on the drawing board)", whereas it means the "representation of the shapes on the earthen floors of the building sites" or the "measurement of the foundation walls on the building site". *Orthographia*, on the other hand, is "the upright image of the exterior view and the shape of the future building painted by calculations not too large", which actually means a *painted or drawn* and reduced elevation.[230]

The mistranslations had far-reaching consequences and led to a whole series of false conclusions by various architectural historians: For example, it is claimed that

- Vitruvius taught the construction of geometric figures on the drawing board using a compass and ruler.[231]
- According to this, construction plans or drawings of floor plans must have been documented in the Middle Ages, as they were supposedly since Vitruvius.
- And finally, it is claimed that *"instructional mathematical or geometrical books for architects and engineers"* existed in the Middle Ages, as erroneously assumed by Uta Lindgren[232] (cf. section 3.5).

However, all of these theses are untenable. Binding summarizes his findings as follows:

> *"Ultimately, from all the Latin words treated, both in Vitruvius and other ancient authors and in the early and high Middle Ages, it is not possible to conclude that scaled building plans existed. Indeed, only reduced, sketchy drawings drawn with the stylus on the abacus coated with wax or dust did really exist."* [233]

The way in which builders measured buildings during the Middle Ages on construction sites has been passed down by different churches. Examples include the German *Corvey Monastery* in the 9th century, the English *Monastery of Vale Royale* in the 10th century, *St. Michael* in Hildesheim (Germany) and *Speyer Cathedral* (Germany) in the 11th century.[234] The procedure essentially followed that of the Roman agrimensors or surveyors, which had already been known since antiquity, and was adopted by the church during the Middle Ages:

Starting from a pin point, a north-south axis, called *cardo*, and perpendicular to it, the *decumanus*, the intersection angle, were drawn. The axis cross was constructed with the help of a device, the groma. The area delimited by parallel lines to the axial cross formed the later space of the building. Then, the bishop or clergyman consecrated the future church with a cross sprinkled with ashes, connecting the diagonally opposite corners. Later, a masonry cord and pegs were thrown out and various measuring instruments such as compass, masonry cord, straightedge, rectangular measures, plumb bob, and plumb scales were used to accurately measure the floor plan.[235]

In most cases, measurements were taken several times to ensure that the angles were rectangular and the distances uniform. However, there is also evidence of inaccurate measurements, for example at *St. Michael's* in Hildesheim, which has deviations of several centimeters between the east and west aisles. In addition, similar to the *Speyer Cathedral*, the transverse axis is not quite perpendicular to the longitudinal axis. After the measurement process, the foundations were excavated and the building was erected.

Measurement errors and inaccuracies that occured during the measurement on the construction site and were discovered later were corrected during the course of construction. In the case of *Speyer Cathedral*, this resulted in the skewing of individual pillars, which can still be seen today.[236] However, the axial curvature does not necessarily indicate a surveying error, but could also have been intentional in the context of medieval urban planning in Speyer, as Erwin Reidinger has determined for several other churches besides Speyer.[237]

For the *Speyer Cathedral*, as for many medieval churches, it is verifiable that there was no planning of the design and shape of the building from the beginning. But there were several "changes of plan" and the form of the building was developed gradually during the building process. It changed over the centuries, e. g. during the transition from Romanesque to Gothic architectural style. Many churches and cathedrals still have Romanesque as well as Gothic elements.

The commonly used term "change of plan" is therefore not necessarily accurate, as it implies that there were "binding" plans from the beginning that were later changed, which is not the case. In contrast, the term "open master plan"[238] used by Manfred Nagl as a basis for construction seems to me to be much more appropriate. It expresses that the cathedrals on the one hand show self-similar, recurring structures and give a coherent impression, but on the other hand they are not homogeneous because of the long construction periods often lasting several centuries.

3.5 Construction knowledge – how architects learned their profession

Was there any education?

"Nothing has been handed down about the education of a master craftsman for the early and high Middle Ages", as Günther Binding notes.[239] There is all the more reason for speculation as to how this might have been done. According to Jean Gimpel, the master builders were taught in the cathedral schools, such as those that existed in Chartres, Paris or Laôn. There, they came into contact with Greek and Arabic science, thus benefiting from the first translations of ancient mathematical works into Latin.[240] Thereby Gimpel gets entangled into a contradiction:

> *"This is not to say, however, that a Villard de Honnecourt or other architects of his time had acquired a profound knowledge of geometry, trigonometry or algebra. The knowledge of the cathedral builders probably derived primarily from practice and experience. Nevertheless, it can be assumed that their contact with these sciences made them more mathematically precise in the preparation of building plans and in the construction of the great cathedrals."* [241]

Gimpel vacillates between two points of view: On the one hand, the architects had received a kind of education in the cathedral schools and had acquired appropriate mathematical knowledge there. But on the other hand, they learned their craft primarily by doing. In other words, an education that was not really an education? Or predominantly practical doing, supplemented by a scholastic-theoretical education? His explanations remain unclear at this point. Last but not least, he also assumes that construction plans must have existed, but were probably destroyed because *"their storage* was *not considered useful"*[242] – an error, as already shown above (cf. section 1.2)

The essence of his argument is this: If plans existed, the architects must have had mathematical knowledge, which they could only have acquired in the cathedral schools or through training. Again, the whole thing hinges on the lost construction plans and the view held by other architectural and art historians:The planning and construction of buildings without drawings in the Middle Ages was unthinkable, and those who could plan must have learned it beforehand in a quasi-mathematical education. In Gimpel's argument, we find the same "indecision" about the existence of written plans that we find in other authors. Binding stated earlier: Despite the lack of evidence for construction plans before the 13th century, it is repeatedly claimed that they must have existed.[243]

From the point of view of ancient know-how about construction and master builders, this seems partly logical. Although we do not know how architects in antiquity acquired their knowledge, Vitruvius made such high demands on their know-how that one could assume that there must have been an "apprenticeship". Vitruvius requires, among other things, that the architect must be theoretically educated and practically or technically experienced,

> *"skilled in written expression, knowledgeable of the drawing pen, educated in geometry, acquainted with various historical events, having listened diligently to philosophers, knowing something about music, not unversed in medicine, acquainted with legal decisions, knowledgeable in astronomy and of the lawful course of celestial phenomena."*[244]

Although Vitruvius placed a high value on the know-how of the master builder, there is no evidence that training in the sense of several years of schooling to impart the necessary knowledge existed in antiquity or the

Middle Ages. The Latin term interpreted by Fensterbusch as "education" can just as well be translated as "instruction".

Considering of the medieval schools and their teaching canon, as well as the transmission of knowledge in oral or preliterate cultures, it seems completely out of the question that prospective master builders in the Middle Ages acquired elements of later usable professional know-how in cathedral schools.

The liberal and the mechanical arts

Cathedral schools were preceded by monastic schools, that provided elementary instruction in reading, writing, arithmetic, and singing. From around the 8th/9th century, cathedral schools were established in Western Europe, largely supported by the reforming papacy of Gregory VII (1025 – 85) and his "Gregorian reform". Gregory VII encouraged the nascent cathedral schools, and there was to be one in every episcopal see, that is, in every cathedral. He did not have in mind a "school for everyone", but rather special training institutes for aspiring clerics who were to acquire the necessary intellectual tools for the ministry.[245]

Cathedral schools existed in Germany, for example, at Cologne, Speyer, Würzburg, Bamberg and Hildesheim, and in England at Exeter and York. In France, they were particularly successful at the places of activity in Reims, Laôn, Tours, Chartres, Orléons and Paris. The schools were directed by the respective bishop, who granted teaching licenses to various scholars who wished to teach.[246]

In France, the cathedral sites became the birthplaces of modern science and of a new, hitherto unknown scientific methodology, based on ancient knowledge that was increasingly reaching the European centers of learning through the translation of many works from Arabic into Latin.

> *"The primacy of science of the cathedral schools in France secured them a top position as places of knowledge transfer during the 12th and 13th centuries,"* notes historian Martin Kintzinger.[247]

Not least, the success of the cathedral schools led to the founding of the Sorbonne University in Paris in the 13th century, the second one in Europe after Bologna. (The rise of the universities, in turn, slowly led to the decline of the cathedral schools from the 13th century onward). The cathedral schools taught the "seven liberal arts" *(septem artes liberales)*, divided into

- the *trivium* with grammar, dialectics and rhetoric and
- the *quadrivium* with arithmetic, geometry, astronomy and music.

The division into the seven liberal arts goes back to the ancient writer Martianus Capella (5th century A. D.), who wrote an encyclopedia about them. For several centuries, they formed the binding canon of knowledge and education for students.

They were contrasted with the "seven mechanical (practical) arts" *(septem artes mechanicae)* in the 9th century by John Scotus Eriugena and in the 12th century by Hugh of St. Victor. These included:

- *vestiaria* (clothing trade, i. e. tailors, tanners, weavers)
- *agricultura* (agriculture)
- *architectura* (building trade, i. e. stonemasonry, masonry, carpentry)
- *militia* and *venatoria* (martial arts, weaponry, hunting craft)
- *mercatura* (trade and commercial activities)
- *coquinaria* (culinary art)
- *metallaria* (forging, metallurgy).

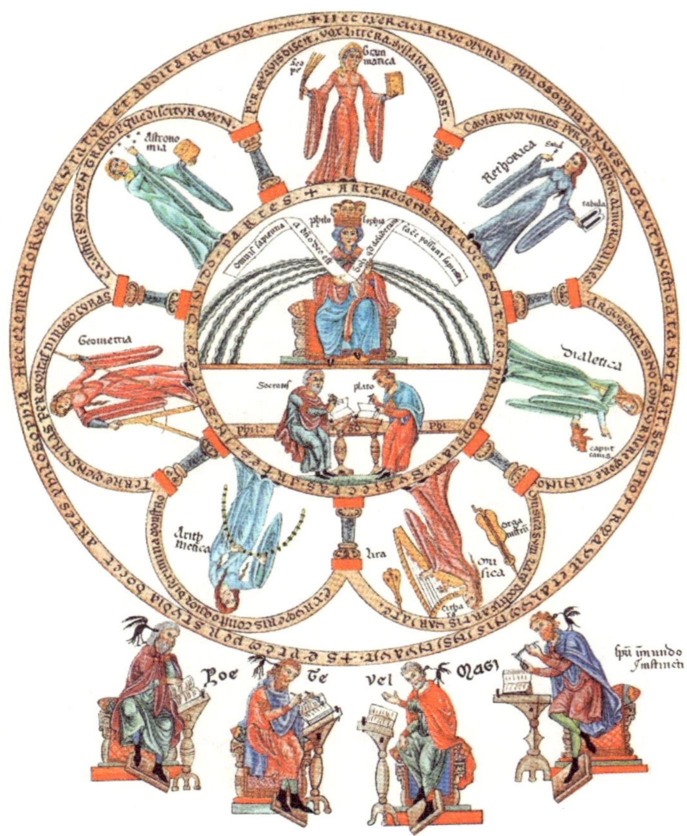

Figure 19: Philosophia enthroned amidst the Seven Liberal Arts – copy of a depiction of the burned original from the *Hortus Deliciarum* of Herrad of Landsberg, Abbess of Hohenburg (c. 1125-1194).
The *Hortus Deliciarum* ("Garden of Delicacies") is the first encyclopedia proven to have been written by a woman, created between 1167 and 1195. This is not the only reason why philosophy is represented as a woman. In oral/preliterate cultures, many things are imagined as personified entities, such as gods or muses in ancient Greece. In preliterate Europe there are still remnants of this, when the seven liberal arts are drawn as female figures, as here. They can also be found as sculptures on many Gothic church portals. Basically oral/preliterate cultures assume a "vitality of the cosmos", which is difficult to understand from the point of view of our present literate culture. We know only "energies", "forces", "abstract (mental) constructs" and "sciences", which we perceive as inanimate, as "factual". - In one petal on the left side, the Geometria is represented with a great compass and a measuring rod.

In terms of prestige, the practical arts were clearly inferior to the liberal arts. The latter are also called free because they could only be practiced by "free men", while the practical arts could also be practiced by the unfree – i. e., by people who were in bonded labor under the feudal system – and served to earn a living.

The practical arts were definitely not taught in the cathedral schools. Thus, educational and practical knowledge remained separate:

> *"No direct path led from the world of the learned university theologian to that of the master craftsman"*, Kintzinger wrote.[248]

So how did medieval master builders acquire or learn their knowledge if they did not complete a scholastic-theoretical education? We must keep in mind that the transmission of knowledge in an oral or preliterate culture is fundamentally different from that in a literate culture. In an oral culture, knowledge is always *experiential knowledge of action,* acquired through practical doing; in literate cultures, on the other hand, it is *teaching and learning knowledge,* acquired through books and instruction. This means:

In oral cultures, people pass on their professional know-how directly by word of mouth, usually from father to son or close relatives, or from master to student or apprentice, without going through a school or training system. People learn primarily by copying and imitating.

In literate cultures, a school and teaching system working with teachers and textbooks – i. e., knowledge in written form – (largely) replaces direct transmission. Instead of experiential knowledge of action, theoretical knowledge in written form derived from practice is passed on. Such knowledge is broader and deeper than purely experiential knowledge because it is based on the know-how of many different masters of a subject and not just on the knowledge of a single person, as is the case with oral transmission. The storage of knowledge on an "externalized carrier medium" such as the book means that transmission no longer depends on the personal presence of the knower.[249]

The dissemination of knowledge in written media also expands the possibilities for choosing a profession. For example, in order to become a baker, merchant or builder, in a literate culture it is not necessary to have close relatives who have the necessary know-how, because it can be acquired through a school with appropriate training. However, this presupposes knowledge of script, reading and writing, as well as the existence of appropriate training institutions and learning media.

Strictly speaking, the oral transmission of knowledge cannot be called "education" in the modern sense. Michael Lingohr points out that before the 15th century, and to some extent even after, the term "architect" should not be understood as designating a profession, but rather as designating a particular function or set of skills.[250]

Throughout the Middle Ages, not only a variety of Latin terms did exist for the *"architect" (architectus, magister operis, rector fabricae, gubernator fabricae,* and *murator),* but they could also refer to different people, each of whom performed different functions in the construction of a building:

- the foreman or manager of the construction site,
- the building craftsman in general, e. g. the stonemason, the bricklayer or the carpenter,
- the person who commissioned the construction,
- the founder of the church (according to the Bible 1st Cor. 3) or

- the building administrator being responsible for the organization of building operations and financial management.[251]

Learning by doing

We know very little about the oral transmission of architectural knowledge, i.e. how a future architect learned his craft in the Middle Ages. It probably followed the path outlined by Barbara Schock-Werner: In the early Middle Ages, from about the 8th century, monasteries and bishops were responsible for the construction of complex buildings, i. e., church buildings in particular, but the execution required craftsmen who were often lay brothers. Individuals who had acquired extensive experience and expertise in construction were also sent to other monasteries to supervise construction activities. On Charlemagne's building sites, for example, monks skilled in construction were assigned to work alongside laymen trained in the craft. In this way, Schock-Werner says, the knowledge available in the monasteries based on the ancient building tradition was disseminated.[252]

> *"The conception, the arrangement of the buildings is determined by clergymen, whose theoretical education did not give them any knowledge of construction. Some of them apparently had the ability to combine this knowledge with practical experience in the construction of buildings. [...] Until the 12th century, there was no systematic and regulated training in the building trade, and analogies with other professions are doubtful. A 'Master' was probably called, who was independently able to build houses with his stonemasons and / or bricklayers. Those who proved themselves were also called upon to build churches and castles."*[253]

> *"An academy, a school of architecture, or even any educational institution where architecture was taught, was not attended even by the brilliant architects of the French cathedrals, and certainly they were no graduates of universities."*[254]

Many professions were "laicized" in the late Middle Ages or the early Renaissance, as can be observed. That is, they broke away from the clerical environment and were performed by "laymen". This process probably also took place among master builders, but we do not know exactly when.

It is known that since the Gothic period, there were workshops (Bauhütten), whose task included the entire organization and financing of the construction process and probably also the "training" of the prospective master builders. Probably most of the workshops were established on the Île de France, i. e. in the heart of France, at the end of the 12th century.[255] One of the first workshops seems to have been that of the *Strasbourg Cathedral*; it was founded around 1190 and first mentioned in 1224. Each workshop or lodge was directed by one or more master builders and included all the craftsmen who worked on the construction. The ideal basis of the workshops was the stonemasaons' brotherhood, a supra-regional organization in which the master stonemasons and journeymen were exclusively organized.

However, our understanding of workshops or lodges and brotherhoods is based mainly on written records of statutes exchanged between stonemasons' brotherhoods from the middle of the 15th century. In Germany, the Strasbourg and Regensburg brotherhoods' statutes were dated 1459 and 1463, respectively. This period coincided with paper's widespread availability and affordability as a writing material. At the same time, the Gothic style had already passed its peak. The simultaneous emergence of the first written workshop statutes, paper availability, and the growth of literacy cannot be seen as a mere coincidence.

The members of the workshops (Bauhütten) obligate themselves to maintain secrecy toward non-members and regarding the private knowledge of their profession, specifically the fundamental principle of construction technique, known as the "gerechter Steinmetzgrund". The secrecy of the workshops was intended to safeguard professional expertise.

Nevertheless, strict adherence to it was never possible, as the required itinerant companionship unavoidably resulted in the spread of knowledge. This was certainly an advantage, because the transfer of construction know-how among the internationally connected workshops[256] also led to its multiplication and further development.

In the early and high Middle Ages, there was no formal schooling or systematic training of master builders, such as in cathedral schools. The germ cells of the transmission of knowledge were probably the masters in the workshops (Bauhütten), often also close relatives. Individuals grew with their responsibilities: Those who demonstrated their skills on the construction site were given the chance not only to work as craftsmen or "performers", but also to take on the planning of buildings, thus fulfilling the function of an architect. For centuries, being an architect was no independent profession, but rather a special task, function or competence of the (stone)mason in the context of a building project. Thus, it was possible for someone who worked as a "senior architect" on one construction site to work as a "craftsman" on the next construction site. It was probably not until the 14th/15th century that the architect became an independent profession.

4. Circles, calculations, and compasses – from the Middle Ages to modern times

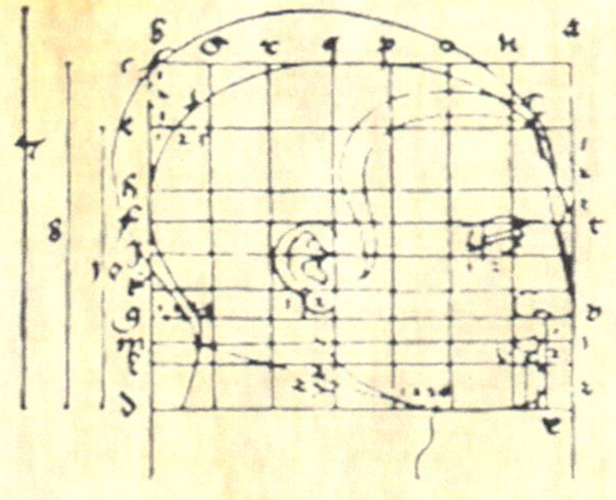

4.1 The medieval knowledge of numbers, geometry and mathematics

Roman and Arabic numerals

After the previous explanations, it seems to be certain that master builders in the early and high Middle Ages could not write and mostly could not read. What was the state of their arithmetic knowledge when they were able to draw orthogonally in a reasonably geometrically correct way from about the middle of the 13th century? Mathematical knowledge seems much more likely to be required for drawing blueprints than for writing. Let's look at the state of knowledge between the 6th and 14th centuries.

After the fall of the (Western) Roman Empire, generally dated to the year 476,[257] and the subsequent migration of peoples, a fundamental change took place in Europe: political instability, an economic recession, the decay of infrastructure (roads) and other factors contributed to the disintegration of established structures, which also affected the educational system. Many of the written works of antiquity, and with them a great deal of knowledge, were lost and did not reappear until the time between the 12th and 15th centuries, by way of Arab culture.

Among the lost knowledge of this period is also that of arithmetic. Only one work was available: *De institutione arithmetica,* a book on arithmetic written by Nicomachus of Gerasa and incompletely translated by Boethius (c. 480 – 524). In the late 10th century, European scholars for the first time benefited from the flowering of Arab culture and were exposed to Arabic knowledge, often in the Spanish city of Toledo, as well as to lost works of antiquity. The French monk Gerbert of Aurillac (c. 950 – 1003) – later archbishop of Ravenna, head of the cathedral school of Reims, and from 999 pope Silvester II – came into contact with mathematics, astronomy and the Arabs' already advanced methods of calculation during his stay in Spain (967 – 970) in Cordoba. He learned the "Indian numerals" that the Arabs had adopted during their cultural flowering after the introduction of paper. These numerals were quickly adopted, especially by Arab merchants, because they facilitated the calculation of larger sums.

Gerbert of Aurillac was the first to introduce the Indo-Arabic numerals together with the astrolabe to Christian Europe. His manuscript and the text have been handed down (cf. Figure 20).[258] He also wrote an introduction to geometry. At that time, the numerals did not have the form we know today; they were modified several times over the centuries until they took their present form.

The introduction of the Arabic numerals in the year 976 does not mean that they were "spread" throughout Christian Europe, as Ifrah claims.[259] Rather, as far as the introduction of new knowledge or the revival of the old one from antiquity is concerned, we have to assume a three-step procedure for the Middle Ages:

1. Introduction of knowledge in the first (Latin) parchments or books
2. Dissemination of knowledge through cathedral schools and, later, universities among an educated minority, preferably among the clergy
3. Dissemination and application of knowledge among the general population, including craftsmen and builders.

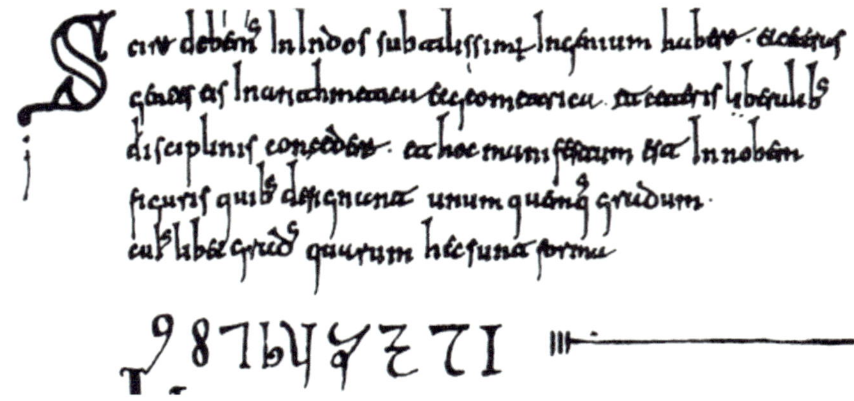

Figure 20: The first appearance of Arabic-Indian numerals in a European manuscript dates from 976 (Codex Vigilanus, San Lorenzo del Escorial, Ms. lat. d.I.2., fol 9v). The Latin text by Gerbert of Aurillac says:

"We must know that the Indians have a very fine character (mind). And that other peoples grant them this in arithmetic and geometry, as well as in the other free disciplines. And this is evident in 9 figures, each of which indicates a step (a level / degree). These are the figures (pictures / forms) of the individual steps: 9 8 7 6 5 4 3 2 1."

(Original in Latin: *"Scire debemus in Indos subtilissimum ingenium habere. Et ceteras gentes eis in arithmetica et geometrica. Et ceteris liberalibus disciplinis concedere. Et hoc manifestum est in nobem figuris quibus designant unumquemque gradum. Cuiuslibet gradus quarum hec sunt forma 9 8 7 6 5 4 3 2 1."*)

Several decades or even centuries could pass between step no. 1 and step no. 2. This was because books were available only in small quantities, were extremely expensive, and, before the invention of letterpress printing, could only be manually reproduced in single copies by order. From step no. 2 to step no. 3, several more centuries passed before knowledge reached the general public through urban schools. For this to happen, the writings first had to be translated from Latin into the vernacular languages, whose importance should not be underestimated. Latin was the language of the scholars, not of the people. Even a literate master builder who could write and read German, French or English would not have been able to read a work in Latin.[260] In addition, a sufficient number of books had to be available. This was achieved with the advent of letterpress printing, which began around 1450 and gradually took hold over several centuries, and the slow growth of book production. Finally, compulsory education was needed to make knowledge available to everyone. Compulsory education was introduced in France in 1793, in England from 1880 and in Germany between 1717 and 1835.

We may assume that master builders in the early and high Middle Ages did not have the knowledge of Arabic numerals for calculating church buildings, even though they were introduced in Europe in the late 10th century.

If at all, builders continued to use the Roman numerals that had been handed down since antiquity, but one could hardly calculate with them in written form. They were essentially used to record the results of calculations carried out objectively.[261] If Roman numerals were used in exceptional cases, the arithmetic operations performed, even for simple additions or divisions, were very often faulty due to the lack of clarity of the long series of Roman numerals.[262]

A well-known *Handlungsbuch der Holzschuher*, a book of accounts kept by Nuremberg merchants in the early 14th century, contains only Roman numerals.[263] This proves that the knowledge of Arabic numerals, which had already existed in Europe since the 10th century, had not yet reached the general public 300 years later and was not used on a daily basis – not even among the otherwise so progressive merchants, who were more open to paper, writing and accounting than the rest of the population (cf. section 2.2).

Confirmation can also be found in the ecclesiastical environment. Tomb inscriptions and construction dates documented in Germany show the spread and slow change from the Roman to the Indo-Arabic numeral system. In the Regensburg Cathedral, whose Gothic building history dates back to 1275, it can be seen that the stonemasons initially used Roman numerals exclusively. In the last third of the 15th century, the first Indo-Arabic numerals appear, in the beginning sporadically, then more and more frequently. In 1464, a new elevator shaft was provided with the same year; furthermore, construction dates and grave slabs with the "new" numerals 1479, 1482 and 1514 are noticeable. But there are also "mixed forms" of dates in Roman and Indo-Arabic numerals, for example, two memorial slabs with the dates "14LXXXVII" for 1487 and "MCCCC88" for 1488.

> *"They attest to how unsure stonemasons and their clients were at first about using the new numerals and how difficult they found it to integrate them into the existing repertoire of signs."* [264]

Apparently, Indo-Arabic numerals were already partially mastered in the two-digit range by the 15th century, but people still had problems with three- or four-digit numerals. This may also be due to the decimal system, which was not used in combination with the Roman counting method.

Roman numerals and their obscurity

"984" – written in Arabic numerals

"CMLXXXIV" – 984, written with Roman numerals

C = 100, M = 1000, CM = 900 (written as "1000 minus 100"),

L = 50,

XXX = 30,

I = 1, V = 5, IV = 4 (written as "5 minus 1").

Writing a Roman numeral correctly seems to be an arithmetic operation in itself, involving both addition and subtraction at the same time.

Up to the number 3, the system works additively; for the number 4, it works only with subtraction from the next higher unit. So 30 is written as "10 + 10 + 10" = XXX, but 40 is not XXXX, but "50 – 10" = XL, where the reading direction is reversed from right to left. From 3999 on, it becomes difficult to write down numbers at all, because the Roman numeral system knows 1000 = M as the highest digit. A jump from 3999 to 4000 therefore does not seem possible in correct notation.

The letters of the Roman numerals correspond in part to abbreviated words (C = *centum* for 100, M = *mille* for 1000), in part to visual halving or doubling of the characters (L = 50 is an angular C written in half), and in part to hand gestures (V = 5 corresponds to an outstretched hand with the thumb and fingers spread apart; X = 10 corresponds to two hands placed side by side).

According to the decimal system for the calculation with Indo-Arabic numerals it needs the zero. But the Occident had to wait another two centuries for the introduction of the zero, which had already been known in the Arab world since Al-Chwarizmi (c. 780 – 835). We owe him mathematically as well as linguistically the "algebra" and the "algorithm". The first breakthrough was made by Leonardus of Pisa, better known as Leonardo Fibonacci. A merchant's son from Pisa (c. 1170–1240), he was taught by Arab teachers in Algiers. In 1202 he wrote his *Liber abacci*. Probably first in the second edition of 1228 Fibonacci wrote:

> *"The new number symbols of the Indians [figuris indorum] are these: 9 8 7 6 5 4 3 2 1. With them and with the sign 0, which is called 'sifr' in Arabic, any number can be written."*[265]

Like Gerbert of Aurillac, Fibonacci adopted the Arabic way of writing from right to left for the numbers. The term "sifr" became "zefero" in Italian, finally "zero", and is of course related to the words "numeral" (German "Ziffer") and "cypher/cipher" (German "Chiffre").

If mathematics were a game of cards, one could call the zero a "joker". From today's point of view, we wonder how it was possible to get along without it at all. It was only possible as long as one used the abacus which had been improved by Gerbert of Aurillac and had replaced the calculation board made of fabric (German "Rechentuch") among merchants. But as far as I know, the abacus was never used by master builders. While there is no evidence of this in the form of illustrations or texts, there is evidence that it was used by merchants who pioneered the use of Arabic numerals and modern arithmetic in Europe.

The introduction of the new numerical system encountered problems. Resistance emerged despite the enthusiastic study of Fibonacci's work by Italian merchants and administrators beginning in 1250 due to the numerous benefits associated with his calculation methods and numerals. For example, in 1299 the council of the city of Florence prohibited banks from using the new Arabic numerals. A comparable reaction occured in Venice, where it was believed that counterfeiting would be easy.

In fact, it takes a significant amount of mental exertion to handle a disparate arithmetic system and set of numbers from the one we have acquired proficiency in. Imagine if today we had to completely abandon the familiar decimal number system in order to write and read all digits in binary code (in a sequence of digits consisting exclusively of 0 and 1) in everyday life. This would be possible, but the mental effort required would be so immense that most people would understandably avoid it. People in the Middle Ages experienced something very similar when they switched from Roman to Indo-Arabic numerals.

North of the Alps, people became familiar with the new numerals much later than the Italians, who were in many ways Europe's pioneers in the Middle Ages. It is said that it took until 1550 for decimal arithmetic to replace abacus arithmetic.[266] This coincides with the life dates of the German mathematician Adam Ries (1492 – 1559), whose well-known arithmetic book *Rechnung auff der Linihen und Federn* ("Calculation on the lines", i. e. with Roman numerals, "and with quill pens", i. e. with Indo-Arabic numerals), written for the first time in the vernacular rather than in Latin, contributed greatly to the final establishment of the Arabic-Indian numerical system in Germany (cf. Figure 21).[267]

Figure 21: Allegory of arithmetic in the *Margarita Philosophica* by Gregor Reisch (1503). Pythagoras (right in the picture) and Boethius (left in the picture) are engaged in a contest in front of the personified Arithmetica. Boethius has already solved the problem by using the modern technique of the "calculation with the quill pen" – with Indian-Arabic numerals on paper using a pen – and looks proudly at Pythagoras. Meanwhile, Pythagoras is still engrossed in his "calculation on the line" with a scowling expression on his face. During the Middle Ages, these men were mistakenly believed to be the creators of both methods of calculation. Arithmetica wears modern looking numbers on her dress. She turns to Boethius while her favor is significant to him, and to the "modern" way of calculating with a quill.

Opponents of decimal arithmetic argued that written arithmetic required a constant supply of new paper, which was expensive, whereas an abacus could be used for a lifetime.[268] We can see from this how important not only knowledge itself is, but also the possibility of constantly having enough affordable writing materials available for its fixation and application. For comparison: In the Arab world, decimal arithmetic and the use of paper as a writing material were already widespread during the 9th and 10th centuries.

Figure 22: Surviving calculation board from the Strasbourg Cathedral Workshop in the 15th / 16th century, which was used for arithmetic "on the line", as shown by the Roman numerals X (10), C (100), and M (1,000). Presumably, calculating on this table saved paper, even though it had long since become commonplace in Europe. Even in the 15th and 16th centuries, it was still common to calculate with Roman numerals. The table was used to keep the accounts of the building administration of the "Frauenwerk" or *Notre-Dame Work Foundation of Strasbourg*. Today, it is exhibited in the *Musée de l'Oeuvre Notre-Dame* in Strasbourg.

Constructive geometry

Gerbert of Aurillac's work dealt not only with arithmetic and the representation of numbers, but also with basic concepts of geometry and the determination of the area and circumference of plane figures. Other 11th-century-scholars also studied geometrical questions such as the relationship between angles, the sum of the angles in a triangle, and the determination of the area of a circle.[269] With the translation of numerous texts from Arabic, mathematical knowledge also took off. For example, the English scholar Adelard of Bath (1070 – 1160) wrote the first complete translation of Euclid's *Elements* into Latin around 1120/30.[270] Previously, only the incomplete translation by Boethius from the 5th century was available. Gerard of Cremona (1114 – 87), the famous founder of the Toledo school of translators, also translated Euclid into Latin.

In addition to writings on scientific geometry, the Middle Ages also saw the emergence of writings on practical geometry in the tradition of the agrimensors, the ancient field surveyors. For example, Hugh of St. Victor (1097 – 1141) wrote the *Practica Geometriae* ("Practice of Geometry"), divided by him into three sections: measuring heights, calculating areas, and calculating the Earth's circumference.[271] In doing so, he probably benefited from Arabic works, especially the writings edited by Abu Bakr on the application of algebra to geometrical problems based on Babylonian knowledge.[272] In his detailed study of the geometrical knowledge of medieval builders, Lon R. Shelby shows that from the 12th century, the distinction between theoretical and practical geometry, initiated by Hugh of St. Victor, became established.[273]

Figure 23: Artfully designed title page script initial P from one of the few surviving copies of Adelard of Bath's Latin translation of Euclid's *Elements,* c. 1309 – 1316, on vellum (MS Burney MS 275 f.293, British Library, London); the drawing is attributed to Master Meliacin.
The Lady Geometria (again personified) holds a square in her left hand and a compass in her right. She is apparently demonstrating how to construct Platonic figures with the compass. To her right is a man – probably the author Adelard himself – who is in animated conversation with her, as indicated by the gestures of his hands. He is surrounded by interested monks, as indicated by the tonsures; they are probably his students.

In the first half of the 13th century, the first independent instructional geometrical book was written that went beyond the knowledge handed down from antiquity: Jordanus Nemorarius (Jordanus de Nemore) (exact dates of life unknown) wrote the *Liber philotegni de triangulis* ("Philotechnic Book on Triangles"), which contained theorems on triangles and their division, about sections of circles and areas between tangents and arcs, on polygons and isoperimetric figures.[274] But we must not assume that this knowledge reached the builders, as Menso Folkerts notes:

> *"Whether these 'practical geometries' were actually applied in practice is difficult to say, because the knowledge of craftsmen and artists was mostly handed down orally."* [275]

Lon R. Shelby demonstrates that master builders applied neither a theoretical nor a practical geometry, but a *constructive* one. This is a "non-calculating" technique that consists of changing geometric figures in a multi-step process. The points, lines and curves needed to solve a problem are created by transformation.[276] The "calculation" of dimensions according to present-day understanding is thus dispensable.

Geometric figures were developed step by step from simple basic figures such as circles and squares, and constructed with simple tools such as straightedges and compasses.[277] In his Sketchbook, Villard de Honnecourt shows how master builders could find such solutions.

As described in works of the 15th century, even the construction of geometric details does not require calculations. This applies to the "Booklet Concerning Pinnacle Correctitude" (in German: *Büchlein von der fialen*

Gerechtigkeit, 1486), the "Booklet on Gablets" *(Wimpergbüchlein)* and the "Geometry German" *(Geometria deutsch*, 1487/88) – all three written by Matthes Roriczer (ca. 1430 – 92) – as well as the "Booklet of Pinnacles" *(Fialenbüchlein)* written by Hanns Schmuttermayer (c. 1487).[278] The "pinnacle correctitude" means the proper design of Gothic ornamental gables in plan and elevation. Roriczer was not only a cathedral architect in Regensburg, but also a book printer. He published his own works printed on paper. His "Booklet Concerning Pinnacle Correctitude"[279] takes a look at the detailed planning of a specific part of a Gothic building, but not at the overall planning of a building. Schmuttermayer[280], a goldsmith from Nuremberg, also dealt with a planning detail, namely the wimpergs.

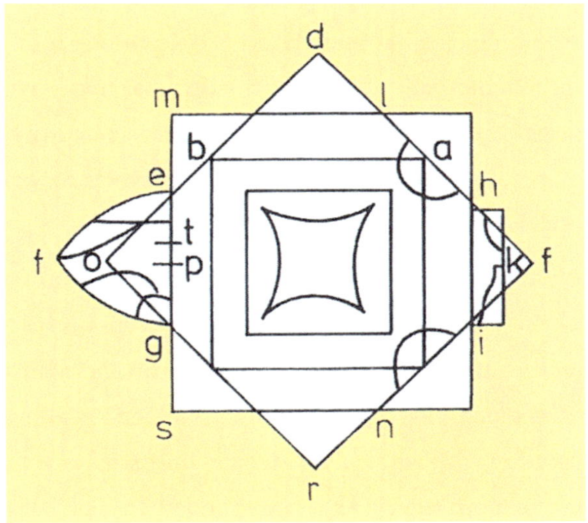

Figure 24: In his *Geometry German* (1487/88), Matthes Roriczer provides very simple instructions for the geometrical development of pinnacles and shows how to enlarge and reduce figures with the help of triangles and squares – an application of constructive geometry. Here is a horizontal section through a pinnacle.

Like Shelby, the historians of mathematics Christoph J. Scriba and Peter Schreiber conclude that it is remarkable,

> *"that the entire designs are feasible without calculations, and that all other dimensions are derived constructively from the initial square."*[281]

The art historian and medievalist François Bucher confirms that Gothic churches are based on a *modular geometric progression* that can be achieved by simple addition and without the use of irrational numbers.[282] This, in turn, corresponds to what we know about members of oral / preliterate cultures: they are often able to solve simple addition problems, but cannot perform complex arithmetic operations.

Arithmetic seems to be a "secondary skill" in all literate cultures, and always follows writing and reading in time, both in the overall cultural development and in the development of the individual. For mathematics is an artificial formal language whose development presupposes that spoken human language has already been written down in binding "signs" or letters (graphemes) and that the individual has mastered this sign apparatus. This largely excludes the possibility that someone can calculate but cannot write or read, since one must first have learned to write and read, in order to operate with numbers.

It is therefore not surprising that the military engineer and theorist Count Reinhard zu Solms (1491 – 1562) in his instruction "A Short Excerpt and Outline to Create a Building" (in German: *Ein Kürtzer Auszug unnd ueberschlag, Einen Baw anzustellen,* Cologne 1556) merely transmitted the calculation with whole numbers and tally sticks for the master builders.[283] The use of notched wood is a method that goes back to the earliest times of mankind and was practiced for a very long time in the absence of writing materials such as parchment and paper, for example for invoices or tax payments.

From this we may conclude that even in the late 15th and 16th centuries, master builders did not, or at least could not, perform calculations. In general, computational knowledge was very "thin" in the Middle Ages and even in the period after:

- The examination regulations of Oxford University of 1408, for example, required only arithmetic with whole numbers.
- In the middle of the 15th century, mathematics was still not required for the *baccalaureate* at the University of Paris, the Sorbonne; the situation was similar at German universities.
- Even after the introduction of compulsory education, arithmetic was not taught at all in some (German) schools, for example in Memmingen, Nördlingen and Überlingen, where it was hoped that "traveling scholars" could occasionally teach the children arithmetic. After all, Bavaria made arithmetic a compulsory subject in village schools from 1548.[284] The situation was similar in other European countries.[285]

The mathematical knowledge of numbers and geometry mostly did not reach the Romanesque and Gothic builders:

- **Mathematical know-how spread increasingly from the 12th century onward, but the texts were written in Latin and were therefore accessible for several centuries only to scholars, not to master builders who only knew their respective vernacular languages. In the vernacular languages, dissemination of such works was slow in emerging with the advent of letterpress printing from 1450 onward.**

- **Roman numerals, hardly suitable for multiplication and division, continued to used well into the 15th century.**
- **Arithmetic was overlooked as a school subject until well into the 16th century.**
- **If you are not able to read and write, you will not be able to perform any calculations except simple additions.**
- **The surviving early architectural drawings of the 13th to 15th centuries show that the geometric figures could be constructed graphically by simple transformation operations without requiring calculation.**

4.2 Passion for compasses – the amazing variety of types

The compass, the underestimated universal tool

According to architectural historians, in the Middle Ages, the same instruments for surveying terrain, buildings, and drawing were available as in antiquity, as evidenced by several illustrations. Notable instruments included

- the gnomon (shadow rod), which is used to determine the noon line for aligning the nave of churches and as a basis for the right-angled axis cross of the nave and transept,
- the alignment cord and wooden pegs for tying it,
- the protractor, which is represented either as a right-angled triangle, but more often as a two-angled angle,
- a measuring rod (modern "ruler"), often 3 to 4 m (= 9.84 to 13.12 ft) long,
- a plumb bob for determining the vertical,
- the archipendulum and
- the compass.

When we speak of "the compass" today, we have in mind a modern, handy tool, namely the compass as we know it from school lessons. The idea also dominates the literature on architecture and art history; three things are assumed:

1. A compass must have a writing tip at one end to apply ink to parchment or paper.
2. Its sole purpose is to draw circles.
3. There is merely one type of compass.

However, these concepts were misguided during the Middle Ages and into the Modern Age. To use compasses on soft writing materials, one tip must be designed as a writing tool, which is commonly a pencil today (invented in the 18th century) or formerly a tool for filling with ink. However, medieval compasses were equipped with only two metal tips, without a writing tip. This type of compass is known as a divider, which cannot be used for drawing.

As already explained, they could therefore not be used on parchment because the writing material would have torn and become unusable. These compasses are designed to work on wood, stone, plaster or the building ground itself, i. e. on *hard* materials.

Almost completely overlooked by modern researchers is the fact that in the Middle Ages there were a number of *different types of compasses* that are no longer familiar to us today and that had many more applications than simply drawing circles.

There was no definitive compass in existence in antiquity and the Middle Ages. Instead, a multitude of compasses with diverse applications existed. In my opinion, the types of compasses and their interaction with other mentioned instruments play a crucial role in understanding the development of construction plans as well as the buildings themselves.

However, reconstructing the specific functions of different compass types during different periods, from antiquity to modern times, and determining when they were replaced or became obsolete by more modern instruments proves challenging.

The compasses of Pompeii

The types of compasses, which were used in the Middle Ages and later, already existed in antiquity. A remarkable collection of compasses can be found among the excavations of Pompeii, the city that was known to have been buried by Vesuvius in 79 A. D. The recovered compasses are now kept in the *Museo Archeologico Nazionale di Napoli*, the National Archaeological Museum in Naples. Their images are readily available online (cf. Figure 25), and they are being studied in Italian research papers.[286]

The different forms of all the compasses suggest that they served different purposes in the past, which are not immediately apparent to us today. In the following I provide an overview of these functions, though it is important to note that this is not an exhaustive list. The historical investigation of the compasses, their application spectra and periods would require a separate work.

As far as I know, Konrad Hecht is the only architectural historian who has decoded the various functions of the compasses on the basis of their formations.[287] However, in my opinion, his attempt is not consistently conclusive nor complete. There are various compass types such as

- *outside calipers,* sometimes also interpreted as "pliers". They were used to measure the diameter of cylindrical objects or other distances,
- *inside calipers* with outwardly curved legs used to measure the dimensions of hollow objects,
- *one-hand compasses,* the exact use of which we do not know today; they must have been designed in such a way as to leave the builder or stonemason one hand free to hold something important,
- *compasses* with settings arcs,
- *compasses* with fixing scews,

- *reduction compasses and proportional dividers,* which will be presented in more detail in the next section,
- compasses with very inwardly inclined legs, whose use still puzzles us today, since the reason for the inclination of the legs is unknown.

Even a cursory examination of this "compass arsenal" reveals that they were not at all useful as engraving or writing compasses on soft materials, but served other purposes.

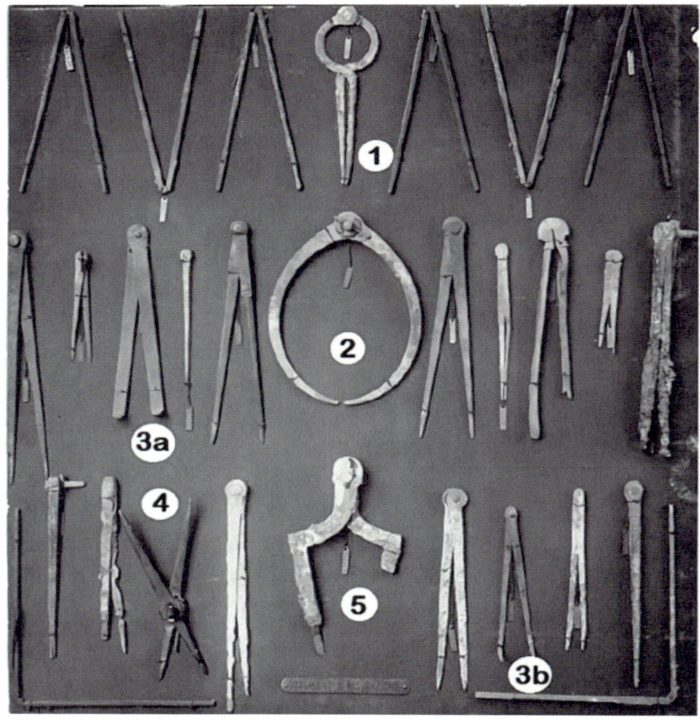

Figure 25: Compasses recovered from Pompeii. No. 1: One-hand compass, similar to the one used as "brand" by master builders in the 13th and 14th centuries. No. 2: Outside caliper. No. 3a and 3b: Inside calipers with outward curved legs. No. 4: Reduction compass with fixed joint. No. 5: Compass with legs bent inwards (caliper?).

In the Middle Ages, the compass was a kind of "universal instrument" that was used for many different tasks on the construction site itself, as well as for drawing on various *hard* surfaces. Many of these tasks are no longer familiar to us today. Above all, the various types of compasses made it possible to simply "capture" distances, as well as the internal and external dimensions of bodies with the two legs, without measuring or calculating them – as we do today.

There are a number of medieval illustrations that clearly illustrate this "capturing" or "taking" of measures and the transfer of distances by using the compass on a protractor or measuring rod. Quite obviously, the compass served, to put it in modern terms, as a "measuring instrument" that led to results without having to mathematically calculate or "count" the measures – a very simple but effective tool.

Figure 26: A copy of a page from Isidore of Seville's *Etymologiae 1-16*, published around 1130 – 1140 in Zwiefalten, Switzerland (own creative redesign and coloring by the author). Shown is the initial G at the beginning of the chapter "Geometria". Clearly recognizable is the person taking a measurement with a large compass on the measuring rod. His clothing, with hat and skirted shirt corresponds to the depiction of a stonemason in Otto of Freising's *Chronica* from the 3rd quarter of the 12th century.

Architectural historians repeatedly point out about Gothic buildings that many measurements were "sufficiently accurate", though not as accurate as we would determine them today. Capturing measures with the legs of compasses may explain why. Of course, there were also dimensional and construction errors here and there that had to be corrected afterwards.

About a hundred years elapsed between the publication of Vitruvius' work on architecture (c. 33 B. C.) and the fall of Pompeii, the excavations of which reveal the many different types of compasses. It is highly unlikely that compasses were developed or invented during this period. They seem to be much older and to have existed in other cultures as well. For example, they are also attested to in ancient Greece, with the three different Greek terms *tornos*, *karkinos*, and *diabētēs*. However, the exact character of these (types of) compasses could not be determined from the texts of the Greek authors.[288]

Vitruvius makes no reference whatsoever to the different types of compasses and their respective range of applications. Vitruvius speaks only of "the" compass (Latin *circinus*), as if there was only one type, and he does not mention any reduced scale construction plans.[289] This, too, is astonishing and shows that neither textual nor pictorial sources provide a complete picture of how builders proceeded in antiquity.

The string compass

One of the different types is the so called "string compass" (or "cord compass"), mentioned in many texts, although no definitive version has been passed down. This tool is used by tightening a rope between two piles and then moving one pile around the other to apply relatively large circles on the building ground. The string compass is mentioned by Vitruvius in connection with the alignment of the foundation on the construction site.[290]

However, some historians of architecture and art, such as Konrad Hecht, question its use in view of the inaccurate results it produces. Cords and ropes can easily stretch, leading to irregular circles and inaccurate measurements in floor plan development. Hecht asserted that even with a church choir's radius of about 25 meters (27.3 yd), string compasses were no longer effective.[291]

However, people found other ways to address this issue: As early as the 1st century A. D., Heron of Alexandria mentioned that the rope was stretched strongly for a long time – either horizontally or vertically by hanging a weight on it. After it achieved maximum extension, a blend of wax and resin was used to condition the rope to maintain its length consistently.[292]

It is unknown when the cord compass perished. Nor does anything seem to have survived about its exact use on the medieval construction site. It seems remarkable to me, however, that it was still in use in the 17th century. In his work "The Labors of Mars, or the Art of War" *(Les Travaux de Mars, Ou L'Art de la Guerre,* Amsterdam 1672)[293], the Parisian engineer Allain Manesson Mallet gives detailed instructions on how to construct regular geometric figures, such as triangles, pentagrams, and hexagons, using cord compasses in open terrain or on a building site (cf. Figure 27).[294] This seems to have served, among other things, for designing fortifications.

From this we can conclude: Anyone who knew how to use such a simple instrument as the cord compass skillfully could elicit far more from it than a circle. And obviously the results obtained were accurate enough for the construction of larger buildings, some of which were still planned on the construction site itself in the 17th century. In the sense of the "constructive" geometry presented in the last chapter, applying the circle served as an aid to derive various geometric figures. The fact that this was still done with the help of the compass until the 17th century may surprise us today. According to the Czech geometry researcher František Kadeřávek, the Egyptians are said to have already accomplished something similar several thousand years ago.

Figure 27: In his work *Les Travaux De Mars, Ou L'Art De La Guerre* (Amsterdam 1720, p. 187), A. M. Mallet demonstrates how a circle (yellow) and a pentagram (blue) are marked out on the construction site by using a string and a beam compass (red).

The great compass

Another typical tool for construction during medieval times was the great compass. Many depictions of construction work using this compass, which stood at a height of around 60 to 120 cm (23 to 46 inches), have survived (cf. Figure 19, Figure 26, Figure 28). These compasses were wooden and their tips were likely made of metal. Like the string compass, the great compass was used to draw floor plans directly on the building site. However, the exact use of the great compass in the Middle Ages remains unknown.

Unfortunately, the literature frequently contains the inaccurate claim that the great compass became "dispensable" in the 13th century due to the appearance of the first drawings on parchment. This thesis was first proposed by Dieter Kimpel and has been repeated by other art historians[295]:

> *"The great compass is replaced by the small hand compass."* [296]

Further, Kimpel asserts that the reduction to the hand circle

> *"is significant in that it marks the transition from 1:1 thinking to scale thinking."* [297]

Günther Binding writes similarly:

> *"Great compasses are depicted only until the middle of the 13th century, when they are replaced by handy compasses (with piercing tips), due to the change from the 1:1 outline on the drawing floor or terrain to the scaled-down architectural drawing."*[298]

This thesis theoretically fits well with the argument that construction plans from about 1250 onward supposedly enabled the planning of buildings in written form, thus making the development of the floor plan on the building site itself superfluous. However, this thesis is wrong in two respects: Neither did scale thinking, which is significantly older, emerge with the handy compass, nor did the great compass disappear from the master builder's toolbox.

There is evidence that the great compass continued to be used for centuries after the first parchment drawing appeared. In fact, its use seems to have been improved well beyond the Middle Ages. For example, Walther Hermann Ryff (Rivius, c. 1500 to after 1548), one of the important German pioneers of the development of architectural knowledge in the Renaissance, shows illustrations of great compasses in his work "The Art of Building or Architecture of all distinguished, necessary and associated Arts. Pure Report and Comprehensive Teaching for the Right Understanding of Vitruv's Doctrine" (original in German: *Bawkunst*

Figure 28: Master builder of St. Albans Church, England, with protractor and great compass (circled in red). Excerpt from a painting by Matthew of Paris, created around 1250.

Oder Architektur aller fürnemsten, nothwendigsten, angehörigen Mathematischen & Mechanischen Künsten. Eygentlicher Bericht und verständliche Underrichtung zu rechtem Verstandt der Lehr Vitruuij, Basel 1582, pp. 424 and 440). Ryff developed, among other things, new simple instruments for the "Visierung" of heights and depths in space, also using the great compass.

Almost a hundred years after Ryff, the illustration of a ground compass is found in the work of Jean François Niceron (1613 – 46), a French theologian and mathematician[299], "Curious perspective or artificial magic of the marvelous effects of optics, direct version" (original in French: *Perspective curieuse ou Magie artificielle des effets mervellieux de l'optique, version directe),* first published in Paris in 1638. The book deals in detail with the construction of perspective.

Due to their size and nature, both the string compass and the great compass could not be used on soft writing materials, but only in open terrain, on stone or wood. These types of compasses were employed until the 18th century, indicating that parchment or paper-based plans could not have existed during that time without rendering these tools useless or inapplicable.

The compass seems to have been as elementary as indispensable for the construction of buildings well beyond the Middle Ages, since all other geometric figures or Platonic solids can be derived from it, especially the triangles (triangulature) and quadrilaterals so often noted by art historians.

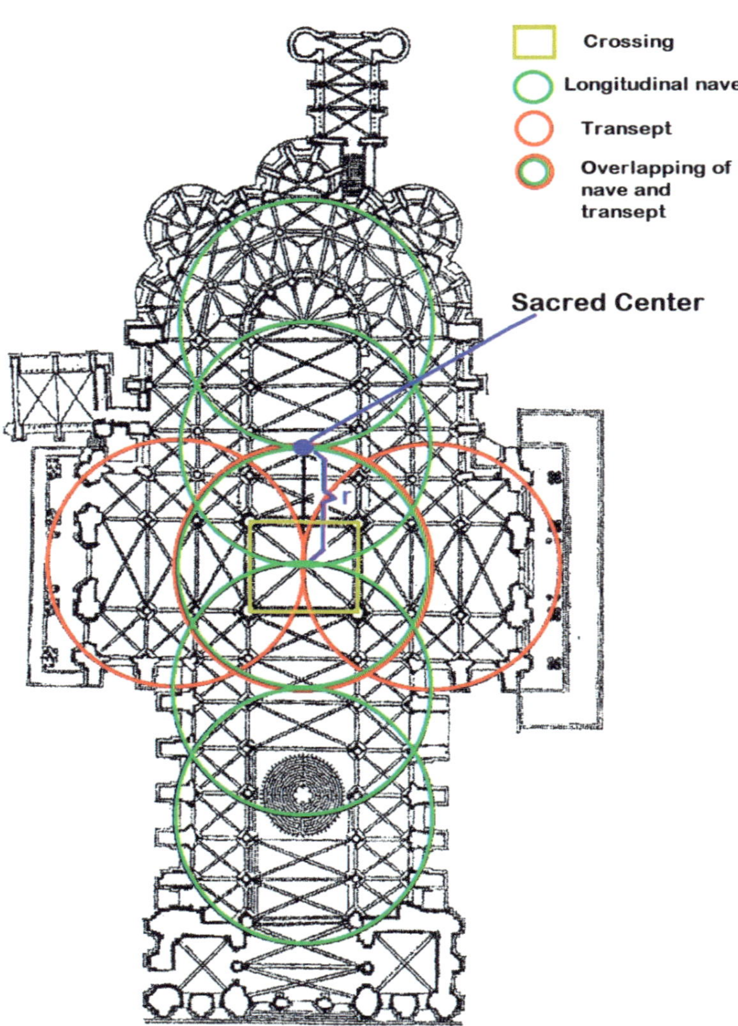

Figure 29: The floor plan of the Gothic cathedral of Chartres (constructed between 1194 and 1220), can be divided into 5 circles of the same radius. The radius of the 5 circles, which completely divide the nave (excluding the north, south and west portals as well as the apse chapels), corresponds to the distance between the sacred center and the middle of the crossing, here marked with "r". (drawing by the author; cf. Klug 2007, p. 63ff.)

The author demonstrated for Chartres Cathedral (cf. Figure 29) that a single stroke of a compass suffices to create the entire ground plan. Specifically, the longitudinal nave can accommodate three circles, while the transept takes two, all with the same radius. The 3:2 ratio of circles corresponds harmonically to the fifth.

The reduction compass and the proportional divider

Were the early parchment drawings true to scale or not? A clear answer to this simple question seems to be easy, but nevertheless historians of architecture and art have not come to a clear conclusion. Early plans from the 13th and 14th centuries consistently did not include scale information. The first plan with scale information is said to have been made around 1420.[300] While some researchers, such as Karl Witzel, believe that scale drawings were unknown in the Middle Ages, others, such as Johann J. Böker and Paul von Naredi-Rainer, disagree. After examining several parchment plans, they came to the conclusion that fixed scales were used on the plans, often according to the duodecimal system (1:12, 1:24, 1:36, etc.), which was common at the time.[301]

Scaled or not, in my opinion, one particular type of compass provides the answer as to how such contrasting theses could have come about, namely the reduction compass, which has been almost completely forgotten.

In contrast to the string and the great compass, which are thought to have ended far too early, the beginning of the use of the proportional divider or reduction compass is considered far too late in the historical literature. It is often claimed that the reduction compass was invented by the mathematician, astronomer and instrument maker Jost Bürgi (1552 – 1632) (cf. Figure 31)[302] and that the proportional divider, a variation of the reduction compass, was invented by Galileo Galilei (1564 – 1642). Both, however, merely developed it further.

In its simplest form, it already existed in antiquity, as the illustration from Pompeii shows (cf. Figure 25, No. 4). That this type of compass was used at least until the 18th century is clearly shown by an exhibition catalog from the *Dresden Zwinger*.[303] The Pompeian compass is said to have allowed reductions in the ratio of 1:2; the compasses from the period from the 16th century onwards also show other scales. Medieval builders must also have used them when they made drawings of a building or part of a building more or less reduced "to scale".

The reduction compass consists of two legs connected by a joint placed between them approximately in the first third. With this tool, you can easily reduce or enlarge to scale, which the author has done by trial and error: Using the two longer legs, one sights two points or a route with the eye in the distance. In this case, the two shorter legs provide a reduction of this distance to a scale that is determined by the seat of the joint between the legs as well as the length of the legs. This mathematically follows the application of the second ray theorem. The reduced distance can then be drawn relatively accurately on parchment or paper. It is also possible to enlarge it by indicating the distance or the points in the distance with the two shorter legs. The result is then drawn on the basis of the position of the two longer legs.

This is exactly how the use of the compass is described in the 16th or 17th century:

> *"Partial or reduction compass with which a line can be divided according to a certain proportion and all sketches, images, bodies can be reduced from large to small and vice versa. This compass consists of two legs of equal length, both of them with a*

piercing tip at the end. The two legs are connected at any point so that they move around an attached pin by opening and closing them."

(Original in German: *"Theil- oder Reduktions-Circul. Vermittelst welchen nach gewißer Proportion eine Linie getheilet, und alle Riße, Bilder, Cörper aus dem großen ins kleine, und vic versa, reduciret werden. Es bestehet dieser Circul aus zweyen gleich langen Schenckeln, davon ieder an beyden Enden mit einer Spitze versehen. Beyde Schenckel sind an einem beliebigen Orte so zusammengefüget, daß sie sich um einen durch beyde applicirten Stifft, vermittelst des Auf- und Zuthuns bewegen [...]."*).[304]

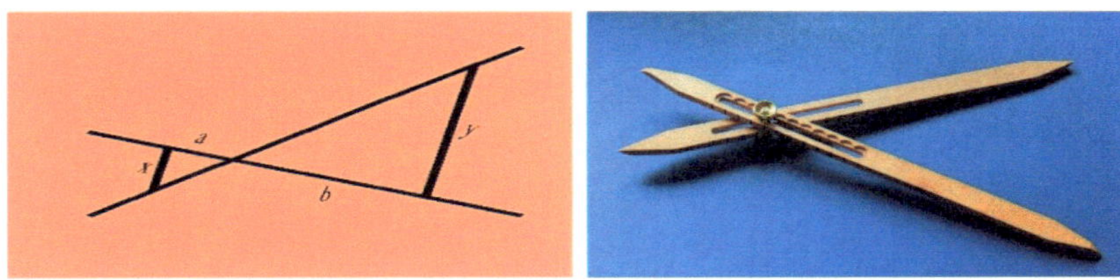

Figure 30: The reduction compass or proportional divider with movable joint (made of wood on the right as a modern scale divider) shows the principle of reduction or enlargement to scale according to the ray theorem a : b = x : y. The compass on the right is set to an enlargement or a reduction in the ratio 1 : 3.

When working with the reduction compass, the "measuring with the eyes" is essential, which in my opinion gives meaning to the term "Visierung" (aiming at a target with the eyes), documented for drawings from the 15th century. The accuracy of the measurement with the eyes and the use of the hands is decisive for the overall accuracy of the scale when drawing a body with the compass. This means that medieval architectural

plans may well have been "appoximately to scale" without explicitly stating the scale and without mathematical calculation; however, the plans were often not one hundred percent "accurate to scale".

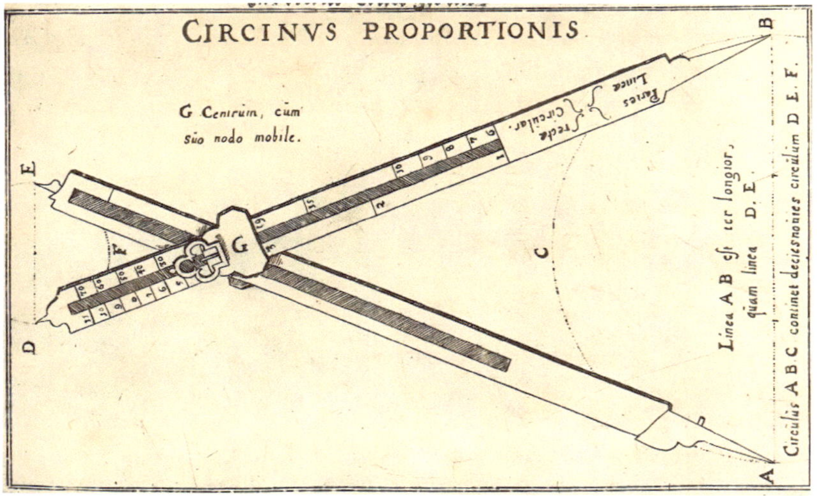

Figure 31: "Circinus Proportionis" by the well-known and innovative German Renaissance mathematician, astronomer and instrument builder Jost Bürgi (1552 – 1632).

The use of the reduction compass provides an explanation for the conflicting estimates of historians as to whether the early plans were to scale or not: they were more or less so, depending on the skill of the reduction compass user or the accuracy of the hand and eye measurements. This also explains the lack of scale indications on the early drawings: Using a reduction compass, one could "read" the scale without having to calculate it or name a numerical ratio. Calculating the scale was not common in the Middle Ages, and in many cases was not even possible for the reasons already explained. But ingenious instruments such as the proportional divider or reduction compass helped to simply measure and transfer measurements as distances by hand and eye instead of calculating them.

The reduction compass was improved in various ways: First, probably in the Renaissance, it was given an adjustable joint instead of a rigid one, so that the leg lengths, and thus the drawing scale, could be varied. Adjustable joints may have been available in the Middle Ages, but nothing has survived. With adjustable joints, the reduction compass is still used by artists today (!), modernly called a "scale divider", sometimes also called a "cranesbill".

Since the Renaissance, reduction compasses have been manufactured by compass smiths, who were often astronomers and instrument makers, too, and who actively participated in the innovative further development of compasses into calculating instruments. Precise reduction compasses are said to have an accuracy of ± 0,1 mm (= 0.0039 in).[305]

Finally, during the Renaissance, the reduction compass was further developed into the proportional divider, which solved an enormous variety of computational tasks. It was found in two different forms: first as a three-legged compass, also known as the golden compass (cf. Figure 32), in the aforementioned work "Art of Building or Architecture" by Walther Ryff (1558, p. 464). The three legs always divide any distance of any length according to the golden section. The author was unable to determine when this apparently lesser-known three-legged shape first appeared; it does not seem to have existed in antiquity or the Middle Ages.

The second form of the proportional divider is found in the treatise "Geometric and military circular operations" (original in Italian: *Le operazioni del compasso geometrico, et militare)* published by Galileo Galilei in 1606. He understood the compass as a *compendium totius geometriae*, a "compendium of the whole geometry", the latter being representative of mathematics.[306] Only a year later, Baldassare Capra of Padua (1580 – 1626) published the next treatise on this type of compass, and similar work continued throughout the 17th and even into the 18th century. In 1781, for example, Michael Scheffelt published his German textbook *Unterricht vom Proportionalzirkel* ("Teaching of the proportional divider") in Breslau.

Figure 32: The three-legged golden compass enables the division of arbitrarily long distances according to the golden section.

The form of the proportional divider handed down by Galileo, Capra, and others consists of two flat legs that open around a fixed pivot, a hinge at the top. One can unfold the compass completely, giving it the shape of a ruler. This type of compass completely lost the function of drawing circles. Soon the pricking tips were replaced by blunt ends.

The "highlight" of the compass is the scales or divisions on the two flat legs. The scales are mathematical function ladders of different functions.

Each function scale can be used to perform different arithmetic operations, such as[307]

- the linea arithmetica: $f(x) = x$,
- the linea geometrica: $f(x) = \sqrt{2}$,
- the linea rectae dividendae: $f(x) = 1/x$,
- the linea cubica: $f(x) = \sqrt[3]{x}$
- and the linea chordorum: $f(x) = 2 \sin(x/2)$.

Without going into the mathematical applications in detail here, the proportional compass made it possible to easily read different values geometrically by taking them off on the two legs with one or two other (one-handed?) compasses, as demonstrated in the following figure (cf. Figure 33).

Figure 33: Artfully designed brass proportional divider (with blunt ends) from the Mathematical-Physical Salon in the *Dresden Zwinger*, made around 1630. The smaller, handy divider with pricking tips is used to read off measurements on both legs of the proportional divider. This is explained in mathematical works of the 18th century, e. g. in Nicolas Bion's (1652 – 1733) French book *Traité de la construction et des principaux usages des instruments de mathématiques* ("Treatise on the construction and main uses of mathematical instruments"), first published in 1709 and in several editions until at least 1752. Bion also illustrated other compasses of the type already found at Pompeii.

In the 17th and 18th centuries, the proportional divider evolved into a *full-fledged analog calculating instrument* that could perform almost any kind of calculation known at the time, with the focus always on the hand and the eye. In modern terms, it almost resembled a pocket calculator. When this type of compass finally disappeared in the middle of the 19th century and was replaced by the slide rule[308], mankind was already on the threshold of the computer age, which began to develop about 80 years later. The slide rule is an instrument very similar to the proportional divider.

In summary, all the different types of compasses or measuring instruments show the

> *"method of representing sizes by geometric quantities (distances, areas, volumes) and performing calculations up to the solution of sophisticated algebraic equations by geometric constructions on these quantities".*[309]

According to Kadeřávek, this method war already common in antiquity and was further developed until the 18th / 19th century.

The "sacred" compass

In the Middle Ages, the compass took on a special, almost religious significance: From 1025 onward, images of God appear in Bibles or Psalters in connection with a compass. This suggests that it was considerd a "sacred tool" that God used to create the cosmos. This can be traced back to the biblical statement: *"You have arranged everything according to measure, number and weight"* (Solomon's Book of Wisdom 11,21) as well as to the idea of God as the architect of the universe, already mentioned in Plato's *Timaios.*[310]

In the earliest illustrations from the 11th century onward, God himself is depicted as a compass, as *Deus Geometra.* His head is identical to the head of the compass (the intersection or joint of the two legs), and the legs extending from his mouth embrace the earth. The earliest depiction of a "god-compass" or "compass-god" is found in the *Annales Colbazenses* ("Yearbooks of the Monastery Colbaz") written around 1150.

In later illustrations from the 13th and 14th centuries, which are more familiar to us today, we meet God as a geometer, who is no longer a compass himself, but holding a compass in his hand, measuring or creating the diameter of the earth with it (cf. Figure 34).

Here, we can already see a development from the "godlike" compass to the "profane" tool with an utilitarian character. Thus, people began to distance themselves from the sacredness of the compass, to see it more "rationally" and to place it in the mathematical sphere – a development that was not completed until the Renaissance. This is analogous to the development of writing (cf. section 2.3), which was also initially considered a "sacred act" before it was profaned. From the 13th century on, the compass was appreciated not only as a geometrical instrument, but also as an astronomical and geographical one, as well as a symbol of Euclidean geometry.[311]

The compass is also mentioned in *Etymologiae* by Isidore of Seville (c. 560 – 636), one of the first encyclopedias to present the entire knowledge of its time, as well as in the well-known medieval work on the arts and crafts techniques by Theophilus Presbyter (1070 – 1127) from the 12th century. However, neither of these works, nor any of the ancient ones, provide details on the types of compasses that existed and how they were used. We only learn that they were made of iron in the Middle Ages, whereas they were made of bronze in antiquity.[312]

From about the 16th century, the compasses may have been made of brass. There were numerous compass smiths and instrument makers who specialized in the production of precision mechanical tools for nautical, astronomical, and construction/engineering purposes. The reduction compass could also have been made of wood in the Middle Ages, since it was only used to carry out a "Visierung", not for drawing on a pad. This would explain why medieval reduction compasses have not survived.

Figure 34: From a Bible moralisée, c. 1215 - 1230, on parchment (Austrian National Library ÖNB Codex Vindobonensis 2554, f. 1v).
God as Geometer: In the Bible moralisée, God holds the compass in his hand as a tool, as if he were using it to create the world . "Bible moralisée" refers to a type of very magnificently illuminated manuscripts of Gothic book illumination in which illustrations of the Bible were juxtaposed with typologically "moralizing", i. e. interpretative, images. The book type of the Moralized Bibles originated around 1220 / 30 at the French court. A total of 14 manuscripts of this type have survived to the present day.

Master builders and their compasses

In line with the shift from the "sacred" to the "profane" compass, master builders began to depict themselves with "their" compasses in the second half of the 13th century. The first known medieval reproduction is the tomb slab of the High Gothic architect Hugues Libergier (1229 – 63), the first builder of the abbey church of *St. Nicaise* in Reims. He is portrayed as a distinguished gentleman who has already left the craftsmanship behind in his outward appearance, with a scaled-down model of the church, a measuring rod, as well as a compass (cf. Figure 12).

Master builders of the late and ending Middle Ages seem to have had a pronounced preference for elevating the compass to their "trademark". This is the case, for example, of Matthew of Arras (1230 – 1350), a master builder active in Bohemia and a representative of the High Gothic period. He chose a compass as his trademark, depicted on the chest of his sculpture in St. Vitus Cathedral in Prague. In the background of the compass, there is a triangle – possibly a reference to triangulation (the development of building proportions with the help of triangles). The same is true of John of Saphoy (c. 1450 – 1500), a master builder and sculptor of the late Gothic period.

The coat of arms of the Ensinger family, a family of master builders spanning several generations in the 14th and 15th centuries, contains no less than three compasses (cf. Figure 35), and they appear to be one-handed compasses with outwardly inclined legs, also known as "pressure compasses" because they open when pressure is applied to the two arches. This type of compass is documented at least until the 17th century.[313]

Sometimes the compass in the Ensinger coat of arms is also interpreted as a pair of pliers, but in my opinion this is not correct. For an architect, a simple pair of pliers is more likely to be a subordinate instrument, rarely used by him and not indicating any particular skill.

Figure 35: Portrait of Moritz Ensinger (c. 1430 – 1483), painted by an unknown artist. The Ensinger family of master builders carried the three-circle coat of arms for several generations. Here, there are only two compasses in the coat of arms, while Moritz has the third compass pinned to his chest like a brooch.

It is noticeable that the compasses in the coats of arms and in the masters' marks of all the master builders mentioned have approximately the same shape; they always seem to be pressure compasses. In addition, they resemble a bronze compass from Roman antiquity, found during an archaeological excavation in the vicinity of Venice, as well as another one from the 17th century (cf. **Figure 36** and **Figure 37**).

Today we do not know much about the different types of compasses and their use in the construction process during the Middle Ages (as well as in the period up to the 18th/19th centuries). It is recognizable that many different identical or similar types of compasses, used from antiquity until well into the modern era, helped to solve calculations geometrically or visually by using circles and distances. They were thus the essential instruments for the very "constructive" geometry that made calculation and measurement in the modern sense unnecessary. The "replacement of the great compass by the smaller hand compass" that Dieter Kimpel and other art historians claim for the Gothic period, did not take place in the 13th century, but continued well into the modern era. This is an additional argument that architectural drawings could not have been a planning medium during the Romanesque and Gothic periods.

In the Renaissance, the need arose to further develop the types of compasses known since antiquity into "real calculating instruments" in order to achieve greater accuracy in construction and engineering planning. This allowed the art of drawing to evolve, and with it the way in which construction plans were represented.

Figure 36: A bronze made one-handed oder pressure compass from Roman antiquity from the *Museo di Torcello,* near Venice. In Italian it is called *compasso a tenaglia*. What might it have been used for? (Author's drawing modified from the original.)

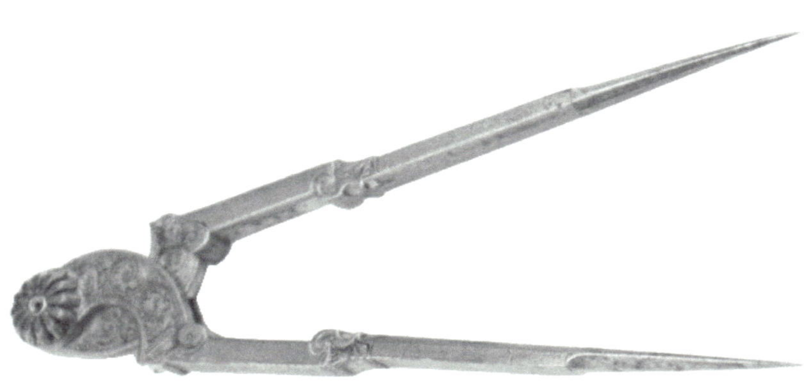

Figure 37: A very similar compass has survived from 1616. The compass is called a caliper and was made by Christoph Trechsler, the famous "mechanicus" at the court of Augustus II the Strong in Dresden. The caliper can be found in the *Museum August Kestner* in Hanover. The only difference to the antique compass is the fact that the two legs have additional joints.

4.3 Advances in the drawing technique of the Renaissance

From the aspective to the perspective

The Middle Ages did not yet know the perspective view. "In perspective" refers to drawings or illustrations designed to create the impression of three-dimensional spatial depth on a flat, two-dimensional surface. It is the form of representation in paintings and drawings that we are familiar with because it has been used exclusively since the Renaissance.

Looking at medieval book illuminations or at depictions of medieval construction (cf. Figure 8, Figure 10), we recognize: They are not in perspective, because they combine different views and partly mix front and side views or top and front views.

A large number of such drawings have been preserved, not only from the European Middle Ages, but also from earlier cultures. They first caught the attention of the Egyptologist Emma Brunner-Traut, who made them the subject of her treatise "Early Forms of Recognition" (original in German: *Frühformen des Erkennens*, 1990). She distinguishes between the *aspective* and the perspective view.

While the perspective view presupposes a *holistic pictorial composition*, this is not the case with the aspective view. In aspective pictures, different elements are juxtaposed in a single image, and the individual elements themselves can each be drawn from different perspectives.

Aspective images are not viewed simultaneously, but element by element[314], without the individual elements being integrated into a whole. In this way, the images are "read one after the other", sometimes even in the direction of writing from left to right. The size and placement of elements follows the *subjective feeling of* the draftsman, what he or his client considers important or significant. For example, in the building scene in Figure 10, the treadwheel is much too large compared to the building, and in the case of the ladder, the side and top views are mixed. In medieval illustrations, high-ranking persons such as bishops, architects, or building administrators are often depicted in large figures, while lower-ranking construction workers are depicted in small figures.

When we look at aspective depictions, we are reminded of children's drawings. In fact, children draw in this way before they have learned to draw in perspective. Brunner-Traut has found that perspective drawings belong to *later* developmental or cultural stages – I would like to add: to *literate* cultures. Oral or preliterate cultures, such as those in Europe before the Renaissance, use the aspective view, juxtaposing elements "additively" and drawing flat, two-dimensional, or only approximately in perspective.

Medieval book illustrations such as Figure 10 and Figure 23 can easily be considered artistic and imaginative. The drawings are made with great care and sometimes have an almost touching effect on the viewer – very similar to children's drawings, which express a lot of feeling, but little distance to the action. Today, we know that in the scriptoria of productive and progressive monasteries the illustrations were not made by the scribe during the reproduction of the books, but that illustrating was an independent profession. There were so-called "rubricators", who added artistic and colored initials and headings, and "illuminators", who were responsible for the pictorial decoration of the books. The approach was effective and based on the division of labor, with different monks, each specialized in his own field, entrusted with the text and the pictorial elements. The fact that the illustrators did not draw in perspective, despite a high degree of routine, suggests that they were simply incapable of doing so, because they were still on the epochal threshold between the preliterate and the literate culture.

The discovery of central respectively linear perspective

Giotto di Bondone (c. 1276 – 1337) decorated the Arena Chapel in Padua in 1305. His frescoes are considered to be the first illustrations drawn in perspective in Europe[315], although they still retained a residue of the medieval mode of representation. Giotto was thus a pioneer in the discovery of central perspective. It creates the perfect illusion of drawing a body as we perceive it with the human eye: All lines thereby meet at an imaginary vanishing point that seems to lie in the depth or distance. About two to three generations of architects or artists worked theoretically and practically on the subject of the central perspective in 15th century Italy, studying Vitruvius in detail.

The discovery of central perspective is attributed to the Florentine artist Filippo Brunelleschi (1377 – 1446), known as the builder of the dome of Florence Cathedral. However, the only evidence is a verbal testimony by Giorgio Vasari (1511 – 1574) in his famous book "Lives of the most excellent Italian architects, painters and sculptors, from Cimabue to the present day: described in the Tuscan language" (original in Italian: *Le Vite de' più eccellenti architetti, pittori, et scultori italiani, da Cimabue infino a' tempi nostri: descritte in lingua toscana),* published in Florence in 1550. He claims that Brunelleschi first used it in 1410 on his panels of the *Piazza San Giovanni* and the *Piazza della Signoria* in Florence. Unfortunately, these panels have not survived.[316] Subsequently, around 1425 his friend and fellow artist Tommaso di Ser Giovanni di Mone Cassai, called Massacio (1401 – 1428), painted the Holy Trinity fresco of *Santa Maria Novella* in Florence in linear perspective. It has survived to this day.

Francesco di Giorgio Martini (1439 – 1501), a sculptor, artist, and architect, explained in his book "Civil and military architecture" (*Architectura civile e militare)*, completed in 1492, that architecture was not only composed of mental concepts, but that these also had to be translated into drawings (Italian: *disegno)*.[317]

Another important pioneer was Leon Battista Alberti (1404 – 72), sculptor, architect, mathematician, art theorist, author and cleric. In several of his writings he attempted to provide a geometric justification for the laws of central perspective.[318] His works are considered the first attempt to establish rules and principles for geometric drawing.[319] In his work "About Construction" *(De re aedificatoria)*, written between 1443 and 1452, Alberti also called for the extensive and careful preliminary planning of a building before its construction. He recommended

> *"'not only in a descriptive way and by drawings, but also by measurements and wooden models, or whatever, to weigh and examine the whole structure and the dimensions of all the individual parts over and over again, according to the advice of the most informed, before tackling anything that requires cost and effort. [...] Here, one can enlarge, diminish, change, renew with impunity, and altogether remodel, until everything comes together properly. [...] Additionally, one can more accurately determine the nature and amount of the future cost [...] by the width, height, thickness, number, extent, shape, appearance, and qua-lity of the individual things, estimating their value and the handiwork of the crafts.'"*[320]

For the first time, the benefits of today's total building design are described here: From accurate drawings and models to the use of materials and labor, all factors must be considered and interrelated in the planning process. In this way, the appearance of the building can be determined in advance, mistakes can be avoided during the construction phase, and costs can be calculated in advance.

Alberti's statement is an important milestone on the way to the complete overall planning of buildings in written and computerized form. This is a turning point, because during the Romanesque and Gothic periods it had been common practice to rebuild churches and cathedrals again and again, to demolish them in parts, to rebuild them again and to change existing plans several times, sometimes when a new master builder took over the job (the so-called "change of plan", although I would prefer to speak of "open master plans"). This led to many important churches being worked on for centuries without being "finished", which of course drove up costs immensely. In the Renaissance, Alberti's statements show a change in thinking for the first time: He advocated planning more thoroughly and over a longer period of time rather than starting work too early, in order to save costs and avoid building mistakes. Today, we take this kind of planning, emerging during the Renaissance, for granted, but at that time it was innovative.

In the 15th-century Italy, the theoretical as well as practical work of numerous artists, many of whom were also architects, sculptors, goldsmiths, artists, engineers and / or authors, led to the development, geometric justification and practical application of central perspective. Its discovery is generally dated to 1410. Around 1443 we find for the first time the requirement that buildings had to be *completely planned in advance*, including not only precise drawing construction plans, but also material and budget planning. These insights reached the countries north of the Alps one or two centuries later.

From central perspective to technical drawing

Although the discovery of central perspective was an important step forward in the development of the drawing art, it is still not sufficient for construction drawings suitable for planning. This is because central perspective has a crucial disadvantage: Since it is used to construct toward a vanishing point as perceived by the human eye, objects farther away are shown in an abbreviated or reduced form. However, builders need to know the exact dimensions of even distant building elements and must not rely on an "guess by eye". In both architecture and engineering, there is a need for distance accuracy, unambiguity, and a type of representation that does not alter the geometric characteristics of the objects depicted.

This is where technical drawing comes in. About 70 years after the discovery of central perspective, it made a decisive advance. The basis is the *orthogonal projection*, also used by the early architects in their drawings from about 1250/75. At first, however, they were only able to depict either a floor plan or an elevation; to combine the two or even to construct a top view or a cross-section, was beyond their capabilities in the Middle Ages. If they wanted to depict several sectional planes at the same time, they simply "projected" them over each other, but only *one* sectional plane was depicted unambiguously and true to distance, the others merely approximately. In the case of oblique views, the oblique side was reduced to two thirds of its width and the missing third was folded behind the front plane.[321] This was a makeshift structure and a common convention on parchment plans since the 13th century.

It was not until the late 15th and 16th centuries that the *multiple orthogonal projection* was developed. It is not yet mentioned in earlier treatises from the 15th century, e. g. those of Alberti.[322] With this projection it is possible to derive the position of a point in a plan unambiguously, provided that it has already been determined on two drawing planes. In this way, distortions and foreshortenings were overcome. Orthogonal plans show true angles and distances or, in the case of scaled plans, true proportions between distances.[323]

With the *multiple* orthogonal projection, *all* elements or features of a building can be identified graphically (cf. Figure 38). In addition, a construction element as well as a building can be shown "simultaneously" from completely different perspectives. It can be rotated and turned in different directions. Not only can every single point on the drawing surface be precisely defined, but its exact position in three-dimensional space can also be derived.

The pioneer of multiple orthogonal projections was Piero della Francesca (c. 1410/20 – 92), artist, art theorist, and mathematician. In his work "About the Drawing Perspective" (original in Italian: *De prospectiva pingendi),* written around 1480, he used the orthogonal projection based on floor plan and elevation. He showed how to transform an orthogonal drawing so that an object could be rotated, tilted and moved. In this way, he demonstrated how to derive other accurate, unambiguous, and sized plans from existing plans or drawings.[324] Francesca inspired, among others, Luca Pacioli in 1509 for his work on "The Divine Proportion", that is, the Golden Section.

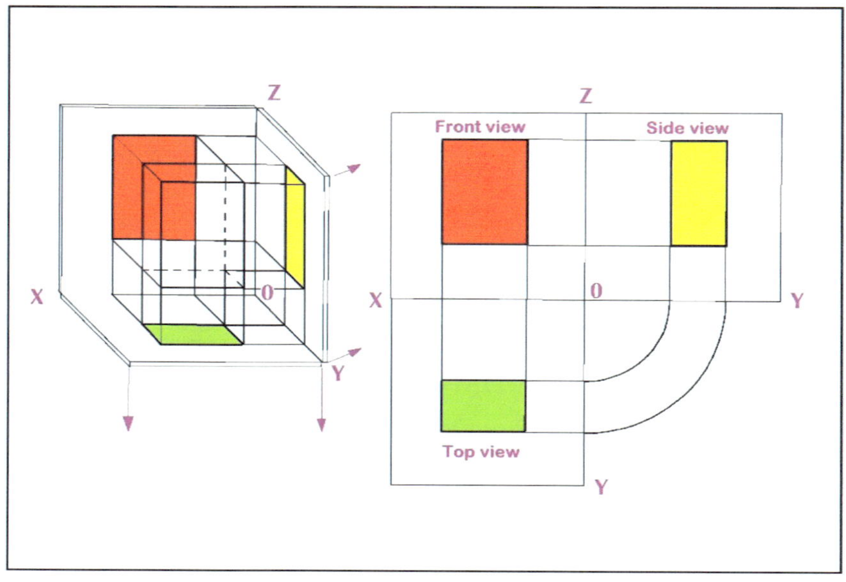

Figure 38: Schematic of the triple orthogonal projection: front, side and top view (or floor plan, elevation, and cross section) intersect at right angles. All section planes are depicted exactly.

Another pioneer was the Italian architect and fortress builder Antonio da Sangallo the Younger (1484 – 1546), who was, among other things, the construction manager of *St. Peter's* in Rome after Raphael's death.[325] Da Sangallo the Younger did not publish any treatises, but he is considered the first known architect to systematically combine different views in his plans when designing a building.[326]

Leonardo da Vinci (1452 – 1519) was also very innovative, not only because of his numerous inventions, his anatomical studies and as a pioneer of painting, but also because of his technical drawings. His detailed studies of machines and buildings reached a level of precision that is unsurpassed even by today's drawings. Among other things, Leonardo is credited with the discovery of isometry, a method of representation that preserves the fidelity of distance.

A highlight in the precise representation of technical relationships is the work "On the Nature of Metals" *(De re metallica)* by Georgius Agricola (= Georg Bauer, 1494 – 1555). He is regarded as the founder of mining science. With his precise technical illustrations and elaborate sectional drawings of the mine, he showed functional relationships and created a high degree of transparency for the reader. His drawings already served as binding execution regulations for the planning engineers as well as for their clients (with regard to bridges, water supply, etc.).[327]

The breakthrough in technical drawing, with its requirements of a true-to-scale, distance-true and exact depiction of any number of sectional planes "simultaneously" came with the *multiple orthogonal projection*, discovered in Italy around 1480. This laid the foundation for architectural drawings, making it possible to plan a building in its entirety. The Middle Ages, however, merely knew the simple orthogonal projection, allowing just *one* sectional plane to be depicted and accepting inaccuracies for all the other sectional planes (if they were depicted at all), i. e. a mix of front and side views.

Not only the orthogonal projection developed decisively in the 16th century, but also other types of projection, which allow a three-dimensional entity to be "exactly" transferred or projected onto a two-dimensional surface. In 1569, for example, the German cosmographer Gerardus Mercator published his famous large world map using the "Mercator projection" named after him, being a significant innovation for geography. It is to Mercator that we owe the word "atlas" in the sense of "geographical collection of maps". Geographers used the same types of compasses as the master builders.

The first architectural models

And the Renaissance brought another innovation: the development of true-to-scale, three-dimensional building models, created between 1350 and 1500. Again, the roots were in Italy. The first full-scale proportional model is documented for the *Sante Maria del Fiore Cathedral* in Florence in 1367. This was a small, walk-in, brick building on a scale of 1:12, approximately 15 m (= 16.4 yd) long and 3,5 m (=3.82 yd) wide.[328]

More common were the portable wooden models, such as those existed for Milan Cathedral shortly before 1400. As Andres Lepik points out, these models require vision and perspective thinking in order to function as a *"proxies for an architectural idea"*. Accuracy of scale is also a crucial criterion for convincing builders and serving as a medium *"on the threshold between imagination and reality"* as a basis for execution.[329] The wooden models are a sign of the increasing differentiation of building design and planning processes during the Renaissance – just as Leon Battista Alberti recommended in 1419: plan more, more thoroughly, and with different media, instead of moving too early into the operational implementation.

The development in Germany

Independent of Antonio da Sangallo, but possibly inspired by Piero della Francesca, the German artist, graphic artist, and art theorist Albrecht Dürer (1471 – 1528) dealt with geometry and perspective in several of his books.

He also developed the multiple orthogonal projection in his work "Instructions for Measuring with Compass and Straightedge, in Lines, Planes, and Whole Bodies" (Original in German: *Underweysung der Messung, mit dem Zirckel und Richtscheyt, in Linien, Ebenen unnd gantzen corporen),* published in Nuremberg in 1525. He was not primarily concerned with architectural plans, but rather wanted to be of service to artists, goldsmiths, sculptors, stonemasons, and other craftsmen.[330] From 1528 onward, his "Four Books on Human Proportion" *(Vier Bücher von menschlicher Proportion)* were printed, taking up the same subject and deepening it stereometrically.

In his work, Dürer was not interested in a theoretical construction of the multiple orthogonal projection, but in *practical instructions* on how to implement it graphically. With his drawings, Dürer is today considered the founder of descriptive geometry, which was only mathematically substantiated much later by the natural scientist Gaspard Monge (1746 – 1818).[331]

Dürer used the term "measurement" (German: *"Messung")* in the title of one of his works. One might wonder why this word appears there, although his drawings are designed in such a way that there was basically nothing to measure. The mathematics historian Jeanne Peiffer points out that in the 16th century, "measurement" was understood differently than it is today, namely in the sense of "perspective construction of complex bodies, mostly polyhedra". For Dürer, the term "measurement" is said to have been the translation of "perspectiva". Accordingly, his method of orthogonal projection did not serve the "measurement" as we understand it today.[332]

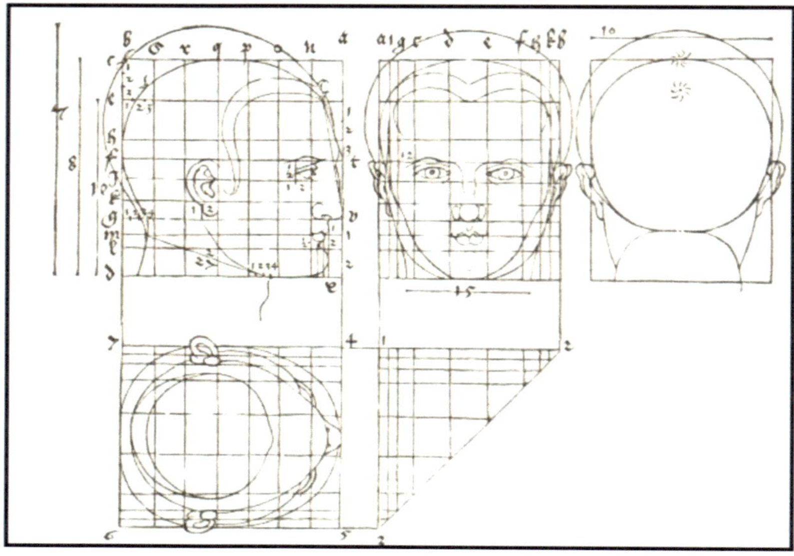

Figure 39: The multiple orthogonal projection from Albrecht Dürer's "Four Books on Human Proportion" (1528), p. 52, which he illustrated using the example of the human head in side, front, back and top views. The triangle shown in the lower right is what Dürer calls a "carryover". It allows the exact right-angled transfer of lines and points defined on two drawing planes to several further drawing planes. It is easy to understand that instead of a head, any other object, such as construction elements or an entire building, can be depicted in this way.

It is significant that the meaning of the term "measurement" changed over time: While today we associate "measurement" with "counting" and "exact calculation", this was not a priority until the Renaissance. "Measurement" stood for "depicting vividly in perspective", very similar to how it was understood in antiquity and the Middle Ages. This corresponds to the "constructive geometry" explained in the last chapter. In general, "exactness" and "calculability" are ideals that developed in the Renaissance (15th/16th century), where they were first put into practice in drawing with instruments such as the more advanced compasses, and were given a mathematical-theoretical foundation from the 17th century onward. This also results in a different understanding of construction plans, even in the 16th century, than we have today – another hint that we should not interpret the horse as a "secret car" when looking at construction plans.

Therefore, it should not be surprising that in the early so-called "Master Craftsman Books" (in German: *Werkmeisterbücher)* of the 15th and 16th centuries – the oldest technical literature by and for architects – by Matthes Roriczer, Lorenz Lacher (or Lechner, ca. 1460–1536) and Hanns Schmuttermayer (cf. Figure 24) there are no references whatsoever to a mathematical determination of the dimensions of structural elements of a building.[333]

Compared to Dürer's works and the other innovative works of the Renaissance, the Master Craftsman Books[334] show a much simpler, but also more rigid way of constructing geometric objects, limited to regular solids. In my opionion, this way of representation was the status quo, already been largely achieved in the Gothic period. It was documented in written form in the Master books for the first time.

After Albrecht Dürer, the versatile German pharmacist, physician, and mathematician Walther Hermann Ryff (Rivius, c. 1500 to after 1548) published several pioneering works on architectural theory. In these books he assigned a supporting function to arithmetic for geometry.[335] Ryff was the first to translate Vitruvius' treatise into German in 1548 and to illustrate it extensively whereby using illustrations of the great compass. His work was a major contribution to the spread of Renaissance architecture north of the Alps. He was also the one who introduced the terms "architect" and "architecture" from Latin into the German language.

In English, the term "architect", meaning "someone who plans something" was used from about 1560; in Old English the term "heahcroeftiga", meaning "high craftsman", had been used earlier.[336] In French, the term "l'architecte" in its present sense has been attested since the 11th century; French, as a Romanic language, probably adopted it early and directly from Latin.[337]

The pioneers of the development of technical draftsmanship such as Dürer and Ryff in Germany, Leonardo, Piero della Francesca and others in Italy, influenced both architecture and engineering, which were still undivided until the 17th century. With the increasing specialization of tasks and the separation of the (military) technical field (fortress construction, weapons development, mining science, mill and mechanical engineering) from the pure art of building (architecture), the architectural profession separated from the engineering profession.[338] Both benefited equally from the innovative drawing methods.

The development of compasses and the art of drawing were mutually supportive from the 15th to the 19th century. In order to improve the art of drawing, to make it more "precise", the types of compasses known since antiquity were refined at the beginning of the Renaissance, including the proportional divider or reduction compass. This led to the development of the central perspective as well as new types of projection, mathematical functions and calculation methods, which in turn contributed to the optimization of the compasses. In many cases, the mathematicians were also instrument makers (compass smiths) and vice versa, i. e. Leonardo da Vinci and Jost Bürgi. Often, they were engineers, architects, artists or cosmographers at the same time.

When the various types of compasses as drawing or calculating instruments had reached their limits in the 18th and 19th centuries, the "quantum leap" to the next instrument occurred a few decades later: the computer. With the computer, the limitation of hand and eye measurement could be overcome, because the focus was shifted to the pure calculation of numerical values, eliminating any inaccuracy of hand and eye.

As an "intermediate solution", the computer was preceded in the engineering and architecture by the slide rule in the mid-19th century[339], which was relatively similar to the proportional divider, as well as the drawing board and other mechanical tools used for technical drawing. The compass, however, was reduced to its simplest function again, that of drawing circles.

From the 18th to 19th century, people increasingly moved away from a visually imaginable "geometric" way of depiction and turned to an "unimaginable", purely numerical way of thinking, which was also based on mathematical theory. It has remained dominant to this day and has been further strengthened by the extensive use of computers. Among other things, this way of thinking also gave rise to irrational numbers, which were unknown in the Middle Ages, operating merely with natural numbers.

The development of "circles, calculations and compasses" from the 13th to the 19th century shows once again that we should not interpret the horse as a "secret car" in the case of the supposedly "missing" construction plans of the Middle Ages. The supposed construction plans could not have existed in the Middle Ages, because the necessary drawing techniques, including the necessary drawing instruments, only reached the required level of development centuries later. Therefore, *overall plans* for the complete construction planning on parchment or paper could not have existed from the 13th to the 15th century and before! Planning was not done by "calculating" building dimensions (or scales) as it is done today, but in a different, simpler, more direct way, using the various types of compasses, which should not be underestimated in their versatile and flexible applications.

4.4 From wheelbarrow to stylus – the change in the architectural profession

The dissemination and codification of the new drawing technique

The development from central perspective to multiple orthogonal projection took only about 70 years, while the simple orthogonal projection had been practiced for several centuries and the drawing based on aspective views even for several millennia. The accelerated development of the art of drawing from the Renaissance onward was probably caused, among other things, by the increasing spread of printed books. They made it necessary to present complex issues in a generally comprehensible and unambiguous way for a large reading public, also in the form of drawings.

In addition, the authors tried to outdo each other in their knowledge and thus also stimulated the rapid development of the art of drawing. With the dissemination of the printed book within a few decades, it is as if *revolutionary new* knowledge, completely unknown in the Middle Ages, broke through, was developed and "potentiated" to an unprecedented extent. This happened not only in the field of architecture, but also in many other areas of knowledge.

However, the dissemination of this knowledge in the various trades and crafts, was much slower and took one to two centuries longer. Barriers included the high rate of illiteracy, even among master builders, the initially enormous cost of acquiring books, and language barriers. The books containing the innovative new knowledge, including the new ways of drawing and projecting, as well as the application of the further developed types of compasses, were written in the respective national languages (Italian, German, English, French), sometimes also in Latin, in German even in the author's own dialect. In fact, the written German developed (from the Saxon chancery language) first with the growing dissemination of books from the early 16th century onwards, largely driven by Martin Luther's translation of the Bible.

Architectural and art historians often fail to consider that architectural drawings, in order to be effective, must fulfill not only planning but also *communicative* tasks. In other words, a few architects whose drawing and planning skills are "highly developed" or even "revolutionary new" can do little. Only when *all* professional colleagues design their building plans in an equal and binding manner on the basis of the same methodology or projection methods innovation will begin to prevail.

Moreover, it is not enough for the architects to develop their plans in a consistent manner, but they must also be interpreted and understood in a consistent manner by clients and, above all, by all those who carry out the construction work, in order to be implemented completely and without errors. This is where their communicative function lies.

In other words, it required the *codification* of the new forms of representation for technical or architectural drawings developed during the Renaissance. Codification is a lengthy process that takes several generations to reach a general "social agreement" that the new methodology must now be applied by everyone everywhere to ensure a uniform standard.

According to Wolfgang Lefèvre, philosopher and historian of science, the knowledge developed in the 15th and 16th centuries about the expedient construction of architectural plans was at first reluctantly accepted by architects, because, after all, they could manage without the innovations.[340] Moreover, at that time, the master builders had not yet become thoroughly literate. Apparently, it is typical of human history that innovations are persistent, slow, and meet with resistance. We already witnessed this during the introduction of paper and the Indo-Arabic numerals, including the zero; it took several centuries for them to become widespread. Other significant barriers to adoption, such as language barriers and high book prices, have already been mentioned.

By the time the Baroque style became established in the 17th and 18th centuries, the multiple orthogonal projection prevailed in architectural plans north of the Alps.[341] It is certainly no coincidence that the first German school of architecture was founded in Braunschweig in 1745.[342]

The earliest evidence that a floor plan was first fixed on a drawing and then applied to the building site is a preserved illustration from the Baroque period in A. M. Mallet's work "The Labors of Mars, or the Art of War" (French original: *Les Travaux de Mars, Ou L'Art de la Guerre*), first published around 1672 (cf. Figure 40). Images of building plans or sketches are not seen in medieval depictions of building scenes.

In Italy, the making and reading of technical drawings was taught as early as 1563 in Florence at the "Academy of Drawing Art" *(Accademia delle Arti del Disegno)*, founded under the patronage of Cosimo I de Medici and Giorgio Vasari.

With the establishment of educational institutions, the innovative knowledge and drawing achieved its codification by being anchored. Through teaching, it became the basis of application for future generations of architects (and craftsmen).

Figure 40: A. M. Mallet shows in *Les Travaux de Mars* (Amsterdam 1672, p. 189) that the layout of a ground plan for a fortified building (outlined in green) corresponds exactly to the previously drawn plan (outlined in red). The architect or the person in charge of the construction shows the plan to a construction worker looking in his direction, thus demonstrating that he is following it. It is obvious that string compasses, among other things, were used to mark out the site.

From the "function" to the "profession" of the architect

Some art historians, such as Barbara Schock-Werner, Dieter Kimpel, and Christoph Stiegemann, believe that a fundamental change in the architect's job description took place as early as the 13th century with the appearance of the first drawings on parchment.[343] Christoph Stiegemann even claims that architectural drawing

> *"emerged soon after 1200 as the new medium that within a few decades revolutionized all planning and building processes in most art genres."* [344]

As explained above, this description is extremely short-sighted, not to say wrong. We must think not in decades but in *several centuries* if we want to do justice to the developments in cultural history.

I believe that the fundamental change in the profession of architecture, in addition to the introduction of plan drawings, lasted until the 17th and 18th centuries. What is meant here is the change from the "function" to the "profession" of the architect. Master builders in the Middle Ages were primarily craftsmen who temporarily took over the construction management, but could also work again as stonemasons or carpenters on the next construction site. This must have changed as soon as plan drawings became central to the construction process. The more detailed the plans became, the less the master builder needed to be on site. He could leave the practical execution of construction to others, while supervising several building projects himself at the same time.

In my opinion, in the Middle Ages this was only partially possible for a few special buildings, outstanding "star architects" or excellently organized and pioneering workshops (Bauhütten) such as that of the Strasbourg Cathedral (*Oeuvre Notre-Dame de Strasbourg, Frauenwerk).* As far as the art of drawing was concerned, and as far as the craftsmen were well instructed on how to put the drawings into practice, the architects may sometimes have supervised several building sites at the same time, but this was certainly by no means the rule in the 13th century.

Apart from suitable writing materials and a developed drawing technique, there was no codification to ensure that the plans were understood and implemented in the same way by all those involved in the construction, even without the architect permanently assisting the craftsmen with explanations. The explanatory role was later taken over by the "foreman" as construction manager. The corresponding German word "Polier" goes back to the French "parler" (= to speak) and has been documented in Germany since the 14th century. Responsible foremen could also become architects themselves, as evidenced by the fact that an entire dynasty of stonemasons, sculptors, and master builders from the 14th century, "the Parlers", carries the word in their surnames.

Only the *codified* construction plan can become a *clear* transmission belt between the building concept and its realization. This development took place north of the Alps from the 16th to the 18th century.

The fact that architects themselves became more and more dispensable in construction and were able to concentrate on planning tasks is a development for which there is increasing evidence from the 15th century onward:

- In 1459, the Strasbourg workshop regulations stipulated that aspiring master craftsmen had to be apprenticed to an experienced master craftsman and had to have acquired knowledge in practice. During the last two years of their apprenticeship, aspiring masters had to learn "correct drawing" in particular. The rules of the workshops (Bauhütten) also obliged the master to implement "Visierungen", provided that he had made them before the start of construction.[345] Apprenticeship as a stonemason lasted four to five years. Those who completed only three years were only allowed to practice masonry. Only those who had served a master for a full four years were allowed to call themselves "stonemason (journeymen)". After the obligatory period of itineracy, they became masters.[346]

- Clients (builders) commissioned plans or partial plans to distant architects without them being present on site. In 1462, for example, the citizens of Ulm ordered designs for the sacrament house of their cathedral from Master Hans Niesenberger, who was working then in the Weingarten monastery. And the citizens of Salzburg had the design for the tower of their main parish church brought from Nuremberg in 1486.[347]
- Some master builders received contractual permission to supervise buildings far apart from each other at the same time, for example Ulrich von Ensingen, who supervised the cathedral builders of Ulm and Strasbourg from 1399 to 1419.[348]
- Beginning in 1516, the Strasbourg masterpiece ordinance also stipulated that plan drawings were part of the master craftsman's examinations.[349]

From the 15th century onward, the architect was increasingly given "planning authority". He could replace all or part of his personal presence with a building plan, while the foreman took over the management of the construction work. When the "master builder" became the "architect" and took over exclusively planning and directing tasks, his job was upgraded, similar to the profession of the long-distance merchant a few centuries earlier. Since then, the architect sits at his desk with "shoes made of lead", just like the merchant, while he leaves the execution of his plans to others.

As the separation between construction design and construction management grew, the professions of practical construction (foreman, bricklayer, stonemason) were separated from the professions of theoretical construction (architect, engineer). As knowledge grew, both professions required increasingly specialized knowledge, skills and a completely different training. The architectural and engineering professions finally became academic disciplines in the 19th century, when architecture and civil engineering separated from each other in terms of both training and content.

In the 15th/16th to 18th centuries, architectural plans and the profession of architecture probably developed and promoted each other, with the codification of technical drawing for building plans, the assertion of the book as a medium of communication, and the establishment of the art of drawing in education.The growing importance of building plans led architects to focus more and more on the conceptual design of buildings, while craftsmen took over the execution of construction. It can be assumed that the historical evolution has been from detailed to general planning – i. e. from less to more complex planning – and not the other way round, as architectural historians have repeatedly assumed.[350]

Figure 41: The master builder of the Renaissance (woodcut by Jost Amman, 1536). The woodcut clearly shows what was expected of a master builder in the Renaissance. In addition to the "practical" instruments such as compasses, protractors and plumb bobs, which the master holds in his left hand, he now also needs "theoretical" knowledge, which he carries in the form of a voluminous book under his right arm. There is another book on the floor with an instrument to carry out a "Visierung" on it. Both together indicate the unity of theory and practice, and lie on the ground to symbolize that they form the "foundation" of the master builder's skill. The woodcut is intended to show that theoretical knowledge and practical action were considered equally important in the Renaissance, as Vitruvius had envisioned in antiquity. But the full realization of this ideal conception of the "educated" architect would not come until the 18th century.

5. Romans, Romanesque, and Renaissance – summary of the results

5.1 A wrong theory

The question of the construction plans in the Middle Ages is essentially focused on three theses, frequently repeated in the literature and building on each other:

1. With the emergence of the Reims palimpsests from 1220 onward, construction plans *"very quickly"* – within a few decades – developed into a *"new planning medium"* and a *"mature carrier of ideas"*.[351]

According to this, numerous plans on parchment must have been produced between 1220 and 1240. However, no plans are documented for the early Gothic period in question.

From the first thesis the next one is derived:

2. Most plans between the 4th and 13th centuries were either lost, destroyed by fire or water, or deliberately destroyed when they were no longer needed. After all, it was *"inconceivable"* that *a* building could be erected without written plans. Plans have been *"indispensable aids at* all *times"* – in Europe at least since antiquity, as documented by Vitruvius.[352]

From the existence of plans as a basis for building design and implementation, the following propositions are derived:

3. Already in the Middle Ages there must have been "training" or "education" for prospective master builders, probably in the cathedral schools and supported by "textbooks" from which they learned geometry and mathematics.[353]

Taken together, these three theses almost form a theory in themselves – and yet they are all based on false assumptions and are not tenable, as I have explained in detail. The development of drawings for planning did not happen "quickly" within a few decades, but very *slowly and continuously* over several centuries, starting with modest beginnings in the early Gothic period.

The earliest plans (Reims palimpsests, Cologne and Strasbourg drawings) were probably made around 1250/60. However, it was not until 1350 that the number of plans increased significantly. Moreover, until the 15th century, the plans did not yet have the character of "construction drawings" as we take it granted today.

They could not do that at all, because

1. Compasses and the art of drawing were not yet developed enough to allow clear projections of three-dimensional buildings with multiple sectional planes onto a two-dimensional surface.
2. The writing material parchment, always scarce and expensive, did not allow precise drawing with a compass, but only freehand and therefore inaccurate sketching along lines and circles that had previously been marked with a few pinpricks. A suitable writing material was not sufficiently available until paper became mass-produced around 1450/1500.
3. Many master builders were neither literate nor numerate until well into the 17th century. Mathematics in the modern sense, allowing complex calculations of various kinds, did not develop until the 17th century.

5.2 How did they really plan?

Throughout the Middle Ages, people continued to use the planning techniques that had been handed down since antiquity: Floor plans were marked directly on the construction site using string compasses, great compasses and other instruments, as documented since Vitruvius, but has been called into question by modern mistranslations of his texts. From about the middle of the 13th century, elevations were increasingly recorded on parchment, although detailed drawings continued to be torn into hard materials such as stone and wood.

The work was simplified, for example, by coordinating the proportions of the floor plans and elevations. The floor and elevation dimensions of Chartres Cathedral, for example, appear to have been derived from a single compass radius. Plans were fragmentary, if they existed at all, because buildings were not "planned in detail" as they are today:

> *"The design process consisted [...] of gradual planning with permanent changes"[354],* as Nagl notes.

Churches and cathedrals were worked on for decades, sometimes centuries. Sometimes existing plans were continued or implemented, sometimes they were completely or partially changed, and some things were realized without a plan. It also happened that plans were carried out on completely different churches than those for which they were designed.

The fact that many cathedrals nevertheless appear surprisingly harmonious in their proportions and that even different architectural styles such as Romanesque and Gothic merge into a unity, suggests that the architects had some kind of "ideal plans" in mind or that such plans were anchored in the collective memory of several successive generations of architects, even if they were not recorded in writing for a long time.

The turning point came with the Renaissance in the 15th century, when Piero della Francesca in 1480 – 70 years after the discovery of central perspective – succeeded in drawing true-to-scale and size-appropriate orthogonal projections with several sectional planes in such a way that it met technical requirements. Various types of compasses, along with the art of drawing, developed into versatile "calculating instruments" within two and a half centuries.

With the dissemination of letterpress printing, the first books with an instructional character for master builders emerged, in Germany, for example, the "Master Craftsman Books" (1486 – 1488), Albrecht Dürer's "Instructions for Measuring with Compass and Ruler" (1525) and Walther Hermann Ryff's "Art of Building or Architecture" (1582). They were preceded by the written regulations of the cathedral workshops (from 1459/63). This helped to establish an "education" for master builders in the modern sense – with a fixed duration and a binding canon of teaching. This included the acquisition of certain knowledge including the art of drawing, i. e. planning on paper.

This development stabilized about two centuries later in the Baroque era of the 17th and 18th centuries. At that time, the drawing technique was finally codified: Exact construction design drawings were now considered binding for architects and all those involved in construction, and they preceded construction. Since then, the architectural profession has developed in the modern sense with its typical planning power. In the 19th century, the education of architects and engineers finally separated, resulting in two different professions.

With regard to the architectural drawings of the Middle Ages, we must correct all our "scales" – but not the scales of the supposedly untraceable plans, rather the standards of our thinking. It is rooted in a highly literate culture based on extensive writing and often, to use Shakespeare's words, "sicklied o'er with the pale cast of thought" to be able to understand how the early master builders, as members of a preliterate culture, constructed their buildings. They had a "passion for compasses" – they built largely without plans, but not unplanned. The term "open master plan" used by Manfred Nagl captures this fact.

6. Appendix

6.1 From A to Z - a cultural and historical chronology

In numerous instances, accurate assertions can be located in the specialized literature on building and art history. However, when these statements are attributed to an incorrect century, they become inaccurate and can result in misconceptions. To provide a chronological overview of the described facts, the following table includes documented dates (though it is not comprehensive).

7th century

From about 650 onward	The last papyrus documents from the Merovingian chanceries have survived.
From about 680 until the 14th century	Floor plans of 4 churches of the "Holy Places" recorded on wax tablets have been preserved and copied for centuries; wax tablets are commonly used as "notepads" for construction planning and metal styli for marking workpieces, too.[355]

8th / 9th century

From about 650 to 750	Decline of papyrus as a writing material; the Islamic world and Europe switch to parchment.
From about 740 onward	The first cathedral schools are established in Western Europe, continuing the curriculum of the monastery schools with the "seven liberal arts".
From about 750 onward	Significant break in literacy: from the Carolingians onwards, the nobility and clergy are predominantly illiterate.[356]
Around 825	Emergence of the St. Gallen monastery plan on the island of Reichenau (Constance Lake); the ideal plan is made buildable by subsequent dimensional inscriptions for the length and width of the church.[357]

10th century

From about 919 onward	With the politically strong Ottonian emperors, the monasteries become the driving force of building activity, art production and the reproduction of books.
Around 976	Gerbert of Aurillac introduces the Indo-Arabic numerals to Christian Europe.

11th century

Around 1000 until 1070	Early Romanesque period: The Michaeliskirche in Hildesheim (starting in 1010), the Speyer Cathedral (starting in 1025) and the monastery church in Limburg an der Haardt (starting in 1025) are built in Germany.
1057	Last verifiable papyrus document in Europe is documented in the Vatican under Pope Victor II (1052 – 57); parchment documents already predominate in the Vatican at this time.[358]
Around 1070 until 1150	Phase of the High Romanesque: The abbey church of Cluny is built as the largest church in Europe.
1088	Europe's first university is founded in Bologna.
	In Muslim-occupied Spain, paper mills are established in Cordoba, Xativa, Seville, Toledo, and probably other cities.[359]
	Documents are ascribed a "magical" or "sacred" character. Charters are kept in reliquaries or sacristies.[360]

12th century

	The cultural flowering of the Middle Ages begins: numerous social, cultural and economic changes; emergence of the Hanseatic League; invention or rediscovery of technical machines that are also used in construction, e. g. the wheelbarrow (1170 - 1250) and the treadle wheel crane (around 1240); increase in the number of water mills, the water power of which is used to drive sawing, grinding, hammering or cutting work by means of the camshaft.[361]
1109	Oldest preserved European document on paper: an edict of Countess Adelaide del Vasto, Regent of Sicily and Jerusalem.
Around 1120	The abbot Peter Venerabilis of Cluny is one of the first Christians in Muslim Spain to come into contact with paper as a writing material. In the 5th book of his "Treatise against the Jews" he characterizes it as "inferior" because it is made of rags.
Around 1120	The English scholar Adelard of Bath writes the first complete translation of Euclid's "Elements" into Latin; further translations follow, e. g. by Gerhard of Cremona.
Around 1130	Hugh of St. Victor makes a distinction between theoretical geometry and practical geometry.[362]
Around 1137	The compass is depicted as a sacred godlike tool ("god compass") in the "Annals of Colbaz Monastery".
Around 1140 until 1200	In France, the era of Gothic architecture begins. It overlaps with the late Romanesque: The early Gothic cathedrals of St. Denis (starting in 1140), Sens (starting in 1140), Senlis (starting in 1153), Laôn (starting in 1155), Noyon (starting in 1157) and Notre Dame de Paris (starting in 1163) are built.
From about 1150 onward	Clearly recognizable increase in correspondence in the countries north of the Alps (documents, political administration, jurisdiction): The number of written records increases tenfold.[363]

1154 until 1164	The files of the Genoese notary Giovanni Scriba, written on paper, have survived.[364]
1180	Death of William of Sens, the first builder of Canterbury Cathedral. He is considered the earliest named medieval master builder in Europe.
Around 1190 until 1200	The first drawings encarved in stone have survived from England (Byland) and France (Chalons-sur-Marne).

13th century

1202/28	Leonardus of Pisa introduces the zero next to the Indo-Arabic numerals in his "Liber abacci".
Around 1200 until 1350	In France, the High Gothic cathedrals of Chartres (1194 – 1220), Reims (starting in 1211), Amiens (starting in 1218) and the Paris St. Chapelle (1244 – 1248) were constructed.
Around 1210 until 1232	The first paper mill on Italian soil was probably established in Genoa, followed by Bologna, Venice, Padua, Lucca, Amalfi and other cities.[365]
From 1225 onward	Early Gothic period begins in the Holy Roman Empire: Construction of the Strasbourg Cathedral.
1228	Cologne is the first city in Germany to introduce an "official scribe" and thus a written form of city administration; within 80 to 100 years, most German cities follow.
Around 1235	Villard de Honnecourt's Sketchbook is created on parchment. Villard, like other book authors of his time, is illiterate; scribes later add legends to his drawings.
Around 1238	Muslim papermaking in Spain is taken over by Christians and Jews after the Reconquista.[366]
1246	The oldest surviving German paper manuscript is the register book of the Passau cathedral dean Albert Behaim, created in Lyon.[367]

1248	Abbot Menco of Wittewierum near Groningen (Netherlands) describes the building concept of a church in words, as no drawing in written form exists.[368]
From about 1250 onward	1) The number of documents quadruples again. 2) Long-distance trade begins to expand: Merchants learn to write and are the first to use papers and account books to transfer goods and money. Instead of traveling themselves, they set up trading bases and networks over thousands of miles.[369]
From about 1250 to 1400	Change in social and legal relations in Europe through increasing written communication and use of legally binding documents that replace the personal presence of those concerned. Sovereigns stop travelling, and the number of court chanceries increases.[370]
1253	In Paris, the Sorbonne is founded as the second university in Europe.
1256	The interest in Vitruvius reaches its medieval peak; his work is copied many times and summarized by Vincent of Beauvais in the encyclopedia *Speculum maius* (in Latin).[371]
Around 1250/1260	Production of the first elevation drawings on parchment (Reims palimpsests, Strasbourg and Cologne plans).
From 1262 until 1289	The first municipal schools are established in Lübeck, Breslau and Hamburg; in some cases there are special schools for merchants' children.[372]
Before 1276	In Italy, probably in Fabriano in the Marc Ancona, the breakthrough to mass production of paper is achieved with the help of water or tamping mills to crush the raw materials. Paper is not only consumed in Italy, but is quickly exported to the Central European countries north of the Alps.
From about 1277 until 1300	First mechanical clocks with hour hands appear.

1284	In the absence of a construction plan, the work to be carried out for the Franciscan church in Provins is described in detail.[373]

14th century

Around 1248 until 1400	Stage of High Gothic in the Holy Roman Empire: construction of Cologne Cathedral (starting in 1248), Altenberg Cathedral (starting in 1248/59), Regensburg Cathedral (starting in 1273), Nuremberg Frauenkirche (starting in 1350) and Ulm Cathedral (starting in 1377).
1305	Giotto's frescoes in the Arena Chapel at Padua are considered the first illustrations in Europe drawn in perspective.[374]
1348	The first French paper mill starts operations in Troyes.
From 1337 until 1453	The Hundred Years' War between France and England gradually brings Gothic church building to a standstill.
Around 1350 until 1500	Phase of the Late Gothic in France and the Holy Roman Empire
From 1350 onward	In Italy, the first three-dimensional building models emerge; the amount of European architectural drawings increases significantly.[375]
From about 1370 onward	Paper is available in Germany, initially only as an imported product from France or Italy.
From 1390 onward	The first German paper mill is opened in Nuremberg; other mills follow in important trading cities: Ravensburg (1391/93), Augsburg (1407), Strasbourg (1415), Lübeck (1420), Basel (1440), etc.[376]

15th century

1410	The Italian architect and engineer Filippo Bunelleschi discovers the central perspective that ushers the Renaissance in Italy (the "Quattrocento").
1419	In his last will and testament, the Viennese stonemason Simon specifies to whom his plans "on paper or on parchment" are to be passed on.[377]
1420	The first building plan to scale has survived from Bologna.[378]
Around 1443 until 1452	Sculptor Leon B. Alberti demands that buildings should be planned in advance, including drawings, materials, and budgeting.
1446	The employment of Hans Puchsbaum as master builder of St. Stephen's in Vienna is made dependent on the submission of a building plan.
1448/49	A drawing, partly on parchment and partly on French paper, has survived for the Collegiate Church of Sainte-Waudru in Mons near Bergen (Belgium).[379]
Around 1450 until 1500	The era of Gothic architecture ends.
Around 1450	Invention of letterpress printing by Johannes Gutenberg in Mayence. He prints his first Bible on both parchment and paper.
1458	For the choir of St. Lorenz's Church in Nuremberg, the separate commissioning of design and construction is documented. The change from the architect as a "function" to the architect as a "profession" begins to take hold.[380]
1459	The first guild rules of the workshop of Strasbourg Cathedral have been handed down in written form. They specify, among other things, the duration and content of the stonemasonry apprenticeship.[381] "Visierungen" are given legally binding character.[382]

1463	The order of the Regensburg workshop has been handed down in written form.
From about 1470 onward	From Maximilian I on, all German emperors are literate again.[383]
Around 1480	The artist and art theorist Piero della Francesca introduces multiple orthogonal projection for technical drawings in his work "About the Drawing Perspective".
1486 until 1488	The German "Master Craftsman Books" appear: the "Booklet Concerning Pinnacle Correctitude", the "Booklet on Gablets" and the "Geometry German" by Matthes Roriczer. Hanns Schmuttermayer publishes the "Booklet of Pinnacles".

16th century

Around 1500	1) North of the Alps, the Renaissance begins. 2) There are already around 1,000 printing houses in 250 places in Europe, some of which have their own paper mills. The demand for paper continues to grow, and at the same time its price drops significantly compared to parchment. This accelerates its spread.[384] 3) There are about 30,000 printed book titles.[385]
Around 1500 until 1546	The Italian architect Antonio da Sangallo the Younger was the first to systematically combine different views of a building in multiple orthogonal projections in architectural plans.
1514	North of the Alps, the first three-dimensional construction model is documented for the Luginsland Tower of the Augsburg city fortifications.[386]
1516	The Strasbourg Master Craftsman's Certificate Ordinance makes plan drawings part of the master craftsman's examination.[387]
1525 until 1528	Albrecht Dürer publishes his "Instructions for Measuring with Compass and Ruler" and his "Four Books on

	Human Proportion". In doing so, he made a significant contribution to popularizing central perspective and multiple orthogonal projection in Germany.
1536	Jost Amman draws the "ideal" Renaissance architect, educated both practically and theoretically (by books).
1548	The mathematician Walther Ryff (Rivius) publishes the first translated and annotated version of Vitruvius' work in German; he introduces the terms "architecture" and "architect" as technical terms into German.
From about 1548 onward	Bavaria makes arithmetic a compulsory subject even in village schools, but it cannot be taught consistently.[388]
Around 1550	Enforcement of decimal arithmetic in Germany, along with Adam Ries' instructional book.[389]
1569	Gerardus Mercator becomes famous for his "great map of the world"; with the Mercator projection, he develops a method for mapping the globe to scale on a two-dimensional image plane.
1582	Walther Ryff (Rivius), a pioneer of architectural development in Germany, publishes his work "Art of Building or Architecture", in which, among other things, the great compass plays an important role.
Until 1599	There are already around 190 to 250 paper mills in Germany; their number continues to grow.[390]

17th century

Around 1600	There are about 150,000 printed book titles (with a circulation of about 1,000 to 1,500 copies each).[391]
From 1606 until about 1850	The proportional divider is further developed by Galileo Galilei and many other mathematicians and instrument makers into a fully-fledged analog calculating instrument.

1618 until 1648	Germany is thrown back a century culturally and economically as the Thirty Years' War rages in the Holy Roman Empire.
1637	Vienna allows its stonemasons and masons who are unable to read and write to have signatures made by scribes on their behalf.[392]
From 1642 onward	Compulsory education is introduced in Germany, for example in Saxe-Coburg-Gotha (1642), Württemberg (1649), Brandenburg (1662), Prussia (1717/36); the number of literate people in the population rises to 10 - 25 %.[393]
Around 1672	In his "Labors of Mars", Allain Manesson Mallet shows how to construct geometric figures in open terrain using a string compass. He uses a plan to guide the ground plan work on the site.
Until 1699	The number of paper mills in Germany has risen to just under 500.[394]

18th century

Around 1700	The Baroque style establishes the multiple orthogonal projection in building plans; it is now "codified" and thus binding for all those involved in construction planning and execution.
1745	Founding of Germany's first college of civil engineering in Braunschweig.[395]

19th century

Around 1830 until 1890/1910	The populations of England, France and Germany become thoroughly literate; illiteracy declines rapidly.[396]
From 1850 onward	Paper production is revolutionized and simultaneously industrialized: instead of rags, wood fibers are used as raw material. Paper is available in sufficient quantities and at low cost.

6.2 Notes

1 Cf. University of Bamberg / AB (2020).
2 Cf. Conrad 1998, p. 75, translated by S. Klug
3 Binding 2015, p. 147, translated by S. Klug
4 Quoted from Müller 1990, p. 19.
5 Quoted from Müller 1990, p. 292.
6 Cf. Bucher 1968, p. 55f.; Müller 2015, p. 16f., 21.
7 Binding 2014, p. 38, translated by S. Klug; cf. Philipp 2002, p. 82.
8 Cf. Bucher 1968, p. 55; Müller 1990, p. 17.
9 Cf. Shelby 1971, p. 146.
10 Cf. Amt 2009, p. 17.
11 Quoted from Müller 1990, p. 292, translated by S. Klug
12 Conrad 1998, p. 76, translated by S. Klug
13 Cf. Gimpel 1996, p. 92.
14 Cf. Booz 1956, p. 67.
15 Conrad 1998, p. 77.
16 Cf. Mazal 1994, p. 123.
17 Gimpel 1996, p. 92, translated by S. Klug
18 Cf. Schneider 2014, p. 110; cf. Booz 1956, p. 69; Neddermeyer 1998, p. 258f.; Schneider 2014, p. 110.
19 Cf. Schneider 2014, p. 105.
20 Cf. Göttert 2010, p. 123.
21 Cf. Wikipedia: Papyrus, URL: https://de.wikipedia.org/wiki/Papyrus (5/12/2020).
22 Cf. Santifaller 1953, p. 27f.; Sandermann 1988, p. 26.
23 Cf. Sandermann 1988, p. 107.
24 Cf. Santifaller 1953, p. 33.
25 Cf. Santifaller 1953, p. 29, 31.
26 Cf. Santifaller 1953, p. 78.
27 Cf. Schmidt 2002, p. 87; Schneider 2014, p. 105.
28 Cf. Bucher 1968, p. 51; Schäfke 1979, p. 49; Eisenlohr 1997, p. 431; Schmidt 2002, p. 87.
29 Cf. Illich / Sanders 1988, p. 48.
30 Cf. Neddermeyer 1998, p. 185, 188.
31 Cf. Buringh / Zanden 2009, p. 42.
32 Cf. Monro 2014, p. 92.
33 Cf. Needham / Tsuen-Hsuin 1985, p. 2, 4.
34 Cf. Needham / Tsuen-Hsuin 1985, p. 52.
35 Cf. Monro 2014, p. 311.
36 Cf. Monro 2014, p. 318.
37 Cf. Valls i Subira 1978, p. 91f., 99f.
38 Cf. Monro 2014, p. 324, 328.
39 Translated by S. Klug, in accordance with Valls i Subira 1978, p. 100.
40 Quoted from Valls i Subira 1978, p. 266.
41 Cf. Sandermann 1988, p. 116.
42 Cf. Valls i Subira 1978, p. 226; Gasparinetti 2006, p. 234f.
43 Cf. Frugoni 2004, p. 74 and Wikipedia: Adelasia del Vasto, URL: https://it.wikipedia.org/wiki/Adelasia_del_Vasto (5/12/2020).
44 Archivesnotaires: Le cartulaire de Giovanni Scriba, URL: http://archivesnotaires.tarn.fr/index.php?id=5281 (5/12/2020).
45 Cf. Sandermann 1988, p. 116, 121; Schneider 2014, p. 110.
46 Cf. Gimpel 1980, p. 9ff.
47 Cf. Sandermann 1988, p. 121.
48 Cf. Neddermeyer 1998, p. 262; Schneider 2014, p. 112.
49 Cf. Schneider 2014, p. 110.
50 Cf. Neddermeyer 1998, p. 258f.
51 Quoted from Binding 1993, p. 200, translated by S. Klug
52 Cf. Binding 1993, p. 205f.
53 Cf. Engelsing 1973, p. 8.
54 Cf. Sandermann 1988, p. 136.
55 Cf. Engelsing 1973, p. 8; Wendehorst 1986, p. 28.
56 Cf. Sandermann 1988, p. 138f., 147.
57 Cf. Sandermann 1988, p. 150, 162.
58 Cf. Bucher 1968, p. 55; Shelby 1971, p. 146; Müller 1990, p. 292.
59 Cf. Bucher 1968, p. 49, 55.
60 Booz 1956, p. 69, translated by S. Klug
61 Cf. Müller 1990, p. 292.
62 Cf. Ast et al. 2015, p. 308.
63 Cf. Engelsing 1973, p. X.
64 Cf. Wendehorst 1986, p. 10.

65 Cf. Wendehorst 1986, p. 13.
66 Cf. Wendehorst 1986, p. 13.
67 Cf. Wendehorst 1986, p. 15.
68 Cf. Wendehorst 1986, p. 17ff.
69 Cf. Engelsing 1973, p. 2.
70 Cf. Wendehorst 1986, p. 22ff.
71 Cf. Engelsing 1973, p. 3, 5, 12, 20.
72 Cf. Engelsing 1973, p. 46, 49.
73 Cf. Engelsing 1973, p. 96.
74 Quoted from Booz 1956, p. 12, translated by S. Klug
75 Cf. Booz 1956, p. 12.
76 Cf. Wendehorst 1986, p. 28f.; Wenzel 1995, p. 196.
77 Wenzel 1995, p. 196, translated by S. Klug
78 Cf. Skrzypcak 1956, p. 109f., 118.
79 Cf. Skrzypcak 1956, p. 28f.; Wendehorst 1986, p. 28; Meynen 2003, p. 199f.
80 Cf. Meynen 2003, p. 200f., 203.
81 Cf. Wikipedia: Francesco Datini, URL: https://de.wikipedia.org/wiki/Francesco_Datini (5/12/2020).
82 Quoted from Meynen 2003, p. 206.
83 Cf. Wendehorst 1986, p. 28.
84 Information of the Museum Holstentor in Lübeck (Germany); Wendehorst 1986, p. 28.
85 Ong 2016, p. 12, translated by S. Klug
86 Cf. Ong 2016, p. 2.
87 Cf. Ong 2016, p. 2, 16.
88 Cf. Illich / Sanders 1988, p. 49.
89 Cf. Bridges 2005, p. 110.
90 Cf. Bridges 2005, p. 111.
91 Cf. Bridges 2005, p. 111f.
92 Illich / Sanders 1988, p. 43, translated by S. Klug
93 Cf. Ong 2016, p. 38.
94 Booz 1956, p. 69, translated by S. Klug
95 Binding 2014, p. 38; cf. also Binding 2015, p. 148.
96 Quoted after Binding / Linscheid-Burdich 2002, p. 87, translated by S. Klug
97 Quoted after Binding / Linscheid-Burdich 2002, p. 90, translated by S. Klug
98 Cf. Ong 2016, p. 39, 43, 46.
99 Cf. Ong 2016, p. 35ff.
100 Ong 2016, p. 14, translated by S. Klug
101 Cf. Binding / Nussbaum 1978, p. 6.
102 Cf. Binding / Nussbaum 1978, p. 2.
103 Quoted from Barnes / Shelby 1988, p. 25f.
104 Rüffer 2014, p. 92, Quoted from Hahnloser, Hans R. (1972): Kritische Gesamtausgabe des Bauhüttenbuches. Graz: Akademische Druck- und Verlagsanstalt, p. 11.
105 Cf. Wenzel 1995, p. 246, 250.
106 Cf. Illich / Sanders 1988, p. 84; Illich 1991, p. 30.
107 Gimpel 1980, p. 140, translated by S. Klug
108 Conrad 1998, p. 105.
109 Brooks 2008, p. 14
110 Brooks 2008, p. 14
111 Brooks 2008, p. 14
112 Cf. Radl 2019, p. 24.
113 Hammer's notebook can be viewed digitally in its entirety at the Herzog August Bibliothek Wolfenbüttel (Germany), URL: http://diglib.hab.de/?db=mss&list=ms&id=114-1-extrav (9/2/2023)
114 Cf. Wikipedia: Hans Meiger von Werde, URL: https://de.wikipedia.org/wiki/Hans_Meiger_von_Werde (9/2/2023); data on his activities in Strasbourg at URL https://www.oeuvre-notre-dame.org/docments/899526/913434/0/2c828812-4ab0-3a65-1a83-0c0bf18a43cb (9/8/2023).
115 Cf. Ong 2016, p. 39.
116 Ong 2016, p. 51, translated by S. Klug
117 Cf. Ong 2016, p. 30, 44.
118 Cf. Rüffer 2014, p. 92.
119 Cf. Binding 2010, p. 468.
120 Schlink 1999, p. 218, translated by S. Klug
121 Cf. Schlink 1999, p. 217, translated by S. Klug
122 Cf. Binding 1978, p. 7.
123 Schlink 1999, p. 220, translated by S. Klug
124 Cf. Ong 2016, p. 87.
125 Cf. Illich 1991, p. 92f., p. 112.
126 Cf. Illich / Sanders 1988, p. 56.
127 Cf. Wendehorst 1986, p. 26.
128 Quoted from Engelsing 1973, p. 1, translated by S. Klug
129 Cf. Wikipedia: Rudolf von Ems, URL: https://de.wikipedia.org/wiki/Rudolf_von_Ems (5/12/2020).
130 Cf. Ott 2000, p. 106.
131 Cf. Bridges 2005, p. 112.
132 Cf. Gimpel 1980, p. 151.

133 Cf. Kimpel 1989, p. 131, translated by S. Klug
134 Cf. Gimpel 1980, p. 130.
135 Cf. Wikipedia: Arthur Upham Pope, URL: https://en.wikipedia.org/wiki/Arthur_Upham_Pope (5/12/2020).
136 Bloom 2001, p. 161, quoted from Gluck, Jay / Silver, Noël (eds.) (1996): Surveyors of Persian Art. A documentary Biography of Arthur Upham Pope and Phyllis Ackerman. Costa Mesa: Mazda Pub, without page reference in original.
137 Cf. Butschek 2006, p. 157.
138 Cf. World in Figures: Illiteracy in Country Comparison, URL: https://www.welt-in-zahlen.de/laendervergleich.phtml?indicator=49 (5/12/2020).
139 Cf. Müller 2002, p. 96.
140 Cf. Bloom 1993, p. 21.
141 Cf. Bloom 1993.
142 Cf. Bloom 2001 p. 174.
143 Cf. Bloom 2001, p. 174f.
144 Cf. Bloom 1993, p. 22, 24.
145 Cf. Bloom 2001, p. 174.
146 Cf. Bloom 2001, p. 193f.
147 Cf. Bloom 1993, p. 27.
148 Cf. Bloom 1993, p. 26.
149 Bloom 1993, p. 27
150 Cf. Bayerl 2013, p. 26f., 70ff.
151 Bayerl 2013, p. 49, translated by S. Klug
152 Cf. Branner 1958, p. 9f.
153 Cf. Branner 1958, p. 18f.
154 Cf. Branner 1963, p. 140f.
155 Cf. Kimpel 1989, p. 121.
156 Cf. Kletzl 1939, p. 13.
157 Amt 2009, p. 17, translated by S. Klug
158 Cf. Binding / Linscheid-Burdich 2002, p. 77f.
159 Cf. Kimpel 1989, p. 122, 132.
160 Cf. Klug 2006.
161 Cf. Binding 2014, p. 13f.
162 Cf. Branner 1963, p. 135; Schock-Werner 2009, p. 190, cf. also Binding 2015, p. 113.
163 Cf. Steinmann 2014, p. 295, 302.
164 Fondation de l'Oeuvre Notre-Dame, no page reference
165 Cf. Binding 2004, p. 68f.
166 Cf. Binding 2006, p. 60.
167 Binding 2004, p. 13 translated by S. Klug
168 Cf. Binding 2006, p. 60.
169 Cf. Binding 2014, p. 21.
170 Schock-Werner 2009, p. 190, translated by S. Klug
171 Gimpel 1996, p. 93, translated by S. Klug; cf. also Binding 2014, p. 41.
172 Cf. Bayerl 2013, p. 53, 78.
173 Cf. Kimpel 1989, p. 123.
174 Cf. Fondation de l'Oeuvre Notre-Dame, and Klein 2001, p. 166
175 Cf. Steinmann 2003, p. 43, 127, 201, 203.
176 Cf. Steinmann 2003, p. 44.
177 Cf. Steinmann 2003, p. 50.
178 Cf. Steinmann 2003, p. 45.
179 Cf. Steinmann 2003, p. 226.
180 Cf. Kletzl 1939, p. 7.
181 Cf. Kletzl 1939, p. 7.
182 Cf. Kletzl 1939, p. 5, 120.
183 Cf. Binding 2014, p. 82.
184 Cf. Kletzl 1939, p. 6.
185 Cf. Kletzl 1939, p. 14.
186 Cf. Binding 2014, p. 28.
187 Cf. Pause 1973, p. 36.
188 Cf. Kletzl 1939, p. 120, 123.
189 Cf. Kletzl 1939, p. 5; Binding 2004, p. 24.
190 Kletzl 1939, p. 6, translated by S. Klug
191 Cf. Kletzl 1939, p. 6.
192 Cf. Booz 1956, p. 67; Gimpel 1996, p. 92; Conrad 1998, p. 76.
193 Cf. Kletzl 1939, p. 6.
194 Cf. Pfeifer 2012, p. 1113, translated by S. Klug
195 Pfeifer 2012, p. 1518.
196 Wikipedia: Visierung (Kunst), URL: https://de.wikipedia.org/wiki/Visierung_(Kunst) (5/12/2020).
197 Cf. Kadeřávek 1992, p. 9.
198 Cf. Schöller 1989, p. 45.
199 Cf. Schöller 1989, p. 39f.
200 Cf. Shelby 1971, p. 142.
201 Cf. Kletzl 1939, p. 14f.
202 Cf. Kletzl 1939, p. 13f.
203 Cf. Binding 2014, p. 28.
204 Cf. Binding 2015, p. 136f.
205 Cf. Booz 1956, p. 70; Binding / Linscheid-Burdich 2002, p. 75; Binding 2014, p. 41.
206 Cf. Wikipedia: Wachstafel, URL: https://de.wikipedia.org/wiki/Wachstafel (5/12/2020).

207 Marquart 2013, p. 10, translated by S. Klug
208 Cf. Marquart 2013, p. 13, 16, 20.
209 Cf. Marquart 2013, p. 22f.
210 Cf. Völkle 2013, p. 14.
211 Cf. Büker 2020, p. 39ff.
212 Cf. Branner 1958, p. 9, 15, 18
213 Büker 2020, p. 67, translated by S. Klug
214 Cf. Pause 1973, p. 38.
215 Cf. Steinmann 2003, p. 49; Völkle 2013, p. 14.
216 Cf. Steinmann 2003, p. 50; Völke 2013, p. 19.
217 Völke 2013, p. 19, translated by S. Klug
218 Cf. e.g. Steinmann 2003, p. 49; Böker / Brehm 2013, p. 24.
219 Cf. Pause 1973, p. 58, 60.
220 Cf. Kadeřávek 1992, p. 14.
221 Pause 1973, p. 61, translated by S. Klug
222 Kadeřávek 1992, p. 23, 28f.; Camerota 2004, p. 197.
223 Binding / Linscheid-Burdich 2002, p. 96, translated by S. Klug
224 Cf. Schuler 1999, p. 243, 248, 264.
225 Binding 2016, p. 196, translated by S. Klug; cf. Binding 2010b, p. 465f.
226 Jakob Prestel, translation in 1959, quoted from Binding 2016, p. 196f., translated by S. Klug
227 Cf. Binding 2016, p. 199.
228 Cf. Binding 2016, p. 206f.
229 Binding 2016, p. 197, translated by S. Klug; cf. also Binding 2010a, p. 153.
230 Binding 2016, p. 198, 200f., translated by S. Klug
231 Cf. Binding 2016, p. 198 with reference to Heiner Knell, Frank Zöllner, Stefan Schuler and John Harvey / Joan Evans.
232 Binding 2010b, p. 459, 465f., translated by S. Klug
233 Binding 2016, p. 215f., translated by S. Klug
234 Cf. Binding 2010a, p. 154-157.
235 Cf. Binding 2010a, p. 153f.
236 Cf. Binding 2010a, p. 157.
237 Cf. Reidinger 2014.
238 Cf. Nagl 2019, p. 21
239 Binding 2014, p. 30, translated by S. Klug
240 Cf. Gimpel 1996, p. 82.
241 Gimpel 1996, p. 82, translated by S. Klug
242 Gimpel 1996, p. 92, translated by S. Klug
243 Cf. Binding 1993, p. 191; Binding / Linscheid-Burdich 2002, p. 80.
244 Vitruvius / Fensterbusch, I.1 ff., p. 23ff. translated by S. Klug
245 Cf. Kintzinger 2007, p. 108.
246 Cf. Kintzinger 2007, p. 120.
247 Kintzinger 2007, p. 113, translated by S. Klug
248 Kintzinger 2007, p. 29, translated by S. Klug
249 Cf. Ong 2016, p. XIII.
250 Cf. Lingohr 2009, p. 56.
251 Cf. Schock-Werner 2009, p. 186; Amt 2009, p. 15; Lingohr 2009, p. 54.
252 Cf. Schock-Werner 2009, p. 187.
253 Schock-Werner 2009, p. 189, translated by S. Klug
254 Schock-Werner 2009, p. 190, translated by S. Klug
255 Cf. Philipp 2002, p. 82.
256 Cf. Schock-Werner 2009, p. 192.
257 Cf. Wikipedia: Untergang des Römischen Reiches, URL: https://de.wikipedia.org/wiki/Untergang_des_R%C3%B6mischen_Reiches (5/12/2020).
258 Cf. Ifrah 1991, p. 529.
259 Cf. Ifrah 1991, p. 529.
260 Cf. Shelby 1972, p. 404.
261 Cf. Ifrah 1991, p. 528.
262 Cf. Wendehorst 1986, p. 30.
263 Cf. Wendehorst 1986, p. 28, 30.
264 De Padova 2021, p. 59, translated by S. Klug.
265 Klein 2014, p. 8f., translated by S. Klug
266 Cf. Schreiber 2002, p. 18.
267 Cf. Klein 2014, p. 10.
268 Cf. Schreiber 2002, p. 18.
269 Cf. Folkerts 2002, p. 26.
270 Cf. Scriba / Schreiber 2000, p. 197.
271 Cf. Scriba / Schreiber 2000, p. 199.
272 Cf. Folkerts 2002, p. 27.
273 Cf. Shelby 1972, p. 401.
274 Cf. Folkerts 2002, p. 28.
275 Folkerts 2002, p. 31.
276 Cf. Shelby 1972, p. 420f.; cf. also Bucher 1968, p. 50.

277 Cf. Binding 2003, p. 906.
278 Cf. Scriba / Schreiber 2000, p. 209.
279 Cf. Roritzer, Matthäus / Reichensperger, August (1845): Das Büchlein von der Fialen Gerechtigkeit: nach einem alten Drucke aus dem Jahr 1486 in die heutige Mundart übertragen und durch Anmerkungen erläutert, URL: http://reader.digitale-sammlungen.de/de/fs1/object/display/bsb10048477_00005.html (5/12/2020).
280 Cf. Wikisource: Hans Schmuttermayers Fialenbüchlein, URL: https://de.wikisource.org/wiki/Hans_Schmuttermayers_Fialenb%C3%BCchlein (5/12/2020).
281 Scriba / Schreiber 2000, p. 213, translated by S. Klug
282 Cf. Bucher 1968, p. 50ff.
283 Cf. Binding 2004, p. 19; Binding 2015, p. 258.
284 Cf. Booz 1956, p. 9ff.
285 Cf. Shelby 1972, p. 397.
286 Cf. Ruggieri 2017.
287 Cf. Hecht 1979, p. 234ff.; cf. also Vollrath et al. 2000.
288 Cf. Shelby 1965, p. 237.
289 Cf. Binding 2015, p. 16.
290 Cf. Binding 2015, p. 10, 33.
291 Cf. Hecht 1979, p. 255.
292 Cf. Binding 2015, p. 33.
293 Completely digitally available at URL: https://digi.ub.uni-heidelberg.de/diglit/manesson_mallet1696ga (University Library of Heidelberg)
294 Cf. Kadeřávek 1992, p. 34.
295 Cf. Binding 2015, p. 94.
296 Kimpel / Suckale 1985, p. 227, translated by S. Klug
297 Kimpel 1989, p. 130, translated by S. Klug
298 Binding 2015, p. 94, translated by S. Klug
299 Cf. Kadeřávek 1992, p. 65, plate 33 from the work of Jean François Niceron: Perspective curieuse, Paris 1638.
300 Cf. Binding 2014, p. 38.
301 Cf. Binding 2015, p. 111; Böker / Brehm 2013, p. 25.
302 Cf. Wikipedia: Reduktionszirkel, URL: https://de.wikipedia.org/wiki/Reduktionszirkel (9/6/2023)
303 Cf. Schillinger 1990.
304 Schillinger 1990, p. 8, translated by S. Klug
305 Cf. Wikipedia: Reduktionszirkel, URL: https://de.wikipedia.org/wiki/Reduktionszirkel (9/6/2023)
306 Cf. Schneider 1970, p. 64.
307 Cf. Vollrath et al. 2000, p. 21.
308 Cf. Schneider 1970, p. 72.
309 Kadeřávek 1992, p. 96, translated by S. Klug
310 Cf. Friedman 1974, p. 424.
311 Cf. Friedman 1974, p. 422f.
312 Cf. Shelby 1965, p. 238f.
313 Cf. Schillinger 1990, p. 26, 56.
314 Cf. Brunner-Traut 1990, p. 82.
315 Cf. Wertheim 2000, p. 79.
316 Cf. Kadeřávek 1992, p. 90f.
317 Cf. Binding 2004, p. 9.
318 Cf. Kadeřávek 1992, p. 90f.
319 Cf. Camerota 2004, p. 176.
320 Binding 2004, p. 16f., translated by S. Klug
321 Cf. Böker / Brehm 2013, p. 25.
322 Cf. Lefèvre 2004b, p. 219, 221.
323 Cf. Lefèvre 2004b, p. 210f.
324 Cf. Lefèvre 2004b, p. 233f.
325 Cf. Lefèvre 2004b, p. 212f.
326 Cf. Lefèvre 2004b, p. 227.
327 Cf. Bayerl 2013, p. 40.
328 Cf. Lepik 2011
329 Cf. Lepik 2011
330 Cf. Lefèvre 2004b, p. 238; Binding 2004, p. 194.
331 Cf. Peiffer 2004, p. 254.
332 Cf. Peiffer 2004, p. 259f., 275.
333 Cf. Binding 2004, p. 17f.
334 Wikipedia: Werkmeisterbücher, URL: https://de.wikipedia.org/wiki/Werkmeisterb%C3%BCcher (5/12/2020).
335 Cf. Binding 2004, p. 19.
336 Cf. Online Etymology Dictionary, URL: https://www.etymonline.com/de/word/architect (7/9/2023).
337 Cf. Aubert 1961, p. 7f.
338 Cf. Popplow 2006, p. 114ff.; Nagl 2019, p. 24
339 Cf. Schneider 1970, p. 71f.
340 Cf. Lefèvre 2004b, p. 232.
341 Cf. Lefevre 2004b, p. 232.
342 Cf. Booz 1956, p. 16; Nagl 2019, p. 24.

343 Cf. Kimpel / Suckale 1985, p. 228; Schock-Werner 2009, p. 190; Stiegemann 2018, p. 68.
344 Stiegemann 2018, p. 68, translated by S. Klug
345 Cf. Kletzl 1939, p. 10, 12.
346 Cf. Booz 1956, p. 18ff.
347 Cf. Kletzl 1939, p. 6.
348 Cf. Kletzl 1939, p. 6f.
349 Cf. Amt 2009, p. 17.
350 Cf. Nagl 2019, p. 46
351 Cf. Kimpel / Suckale 1985, p. 228; Schock-Werner 2009, p. 190; Stiegemann 2018, p. 68; translated by S. Klug
352 Cf. Booz 1956, p. 67; Gimpel 1996, p. 92; Conrad 1998, p. 75, translated by S. Klug
353 Cf. Gimpel 1996, p. 82; Binding 2010b, p. 459, 465f. with reference to Uta Lindgren, translated by S. Klug
354 Nagl 2019, p. 46, translated by S. Klug
355 Cf. Binding 2014, p. 41.
356 Cf. Wendehorst 1986, p. 13.
357 Cf. Binding 2014, p. 42.
358 Cf. Santifaller 1953, p. 88f.
359 Cf. Valls i Subira 1978, p. 91ff.
360 Cf. Illich / Sanders 1988, p. 49.
361 Cf. Gimpel 1980, p. 9ff.
362 Cf. Shelby 1972, p. 401.
363 Cf. Illich / Sanders 1988, p. 48; Neddermeyer 1998, p. 185ff.
364 Cf. Archivesnotaires: Le cartulaire de Giovanni Scriba, URL: http://archivesnotaires.tarn.fr/index.php?id=5281 (5/12/2020).
365 Cf. Valls i Subira 1978, p. 226; Gasparinetti 2006, p. 234f.
366 Cf. Sandermann 1988, p. 116.
367 Cf. Sandermann 1988, p. 116; Schneider 2014, p. 110.
368 Cf. Binding 2014, p. 41.
369 Cf. Meynen 2003.
370 Cf. Illich / Sanders 1988, p. 43.
371 Cf. Schuler 1999, p. 243ff.
372 Cf. Booz 1956, p. 10; Wendehorst 1986, p. 28.
373 Cf. Binding 2014, p. 41.
374 Cf. Wertheim 2000, p. 79.
375 Cf. Shelby 1971, p. 146; Amt 2009, p. 18.
376 Cf. Sandermann 1988, p. 121.
377 Cf. Binding 1993, p. 200.
378 Cf. Bucher 1968, p. 55; Müller 1990, p. 17.
379 Cf. Binding 1993, p. 205f.
380 Cf. Amt 2009; p. 16.
381 Cf. Booz 1956, p. 17f.; Binding 2014, p. 30.
382 Cf. Amt 2009, p. 17.
383 Cf. Wendehorst 1986, p. 17ff.
384 Cf. Sandermann 1988, p. 136.
385 Cf. Bayerl 2013, p. 95.
386 Cf. Amt 2009, p. 18.
387 Cf. Amt 2009, p. 17.
388 Cf. Booz 1956, p. 11.
389 Cf. Schreiber 2002, p. 18.
390 Cf. Sandermann 1988, p. 121; Bayerl 2013, p. 94.
391 Cf. Bayerl 2013, p. 95 (from Michael North).
392 Cf. Booz 1956, p. 12.
393 Cf. Engelsing 1973, p. 46ff.
394 Cf. Bayerl 2013, p. 94.
395 Cf. Booz 1956, p. 16.
396 Cf. Engelsing 1973, p. 96.

6.3 Bibliography

Amt, Stefan (2009): "Von Vitruv bis zur Moderne – Die Entwicklung des Architektenberufes." In: Johannes, Ralph (Ed.): Entwerfen. Architektenausbildung in Europa von Vitruv bis Mitte des 20. Jahrhunderts. Geschichte – Theorie – Praxis. Hamburg: Junius, pp. 10–45.

Ast, Rodney / Jördens, Andrea / Quack, Joachim F. / Sarri, Antonia (2015): "Papyrus." In: Thomas Meier / Michael R. Ott / Rebecca Sauer (Eds.): Materiale Textkulturen. Konzepte – Materialien – Praktiken. Bd. 1. Berlin / Boston / München: De Gruyter, pp. 307–322. URL: https://www.degruyter.com/downloadpdf/books/9783110371291/9783110371291.307/9783110371291.307.pdf (04/06/2018).

Aubert, Marcel (1961): "La construction du Moyen Age." In: Bulletin Monumental, tome 119, n°1. pp. 7–42. URL: https://www.persee.fr/doc/bulmo_0007-473x_1961_num_119_1_3905 (09/07/2023).

Barnes Junior, Carl-F. / Shelby, Ron (1988): "The Codicology of the Portfolio of Villard de Honnecourt." In: Scriptorium, Tome 42 n°1, 1988. pp. 20-48. URL: https://www.persee.fr/doc/scrip_0036-9772_1988_num_42_1_2002 (09/13/2023).

Bayerl, Günter (2013): Technik in Mittelalter und Früher Neuzeit. Stuttgart: Theiss.

Binding, Günther / Nussbaum, Norbert (1978): Der mittelalterliche Baubetrieb nördlich der Alpen in zeitgenössischen Darstellungen. Darmstadt: Wissenschaftliche Buchgesellschaft.

Binding, Günther (1993): Baubetrieb im Mittelalter. Darmstadt: Wissenschaftliche Buchgesellschaft.

Binding, Günther (1999): *"In mente conceptum* – seit wann gibt es Baupläne?" In: Kozok, Maike (Ed.): Architektur – Struktur – Symbol. Streifzüge durch die Architekturgeschichte von der Antike bis zur Gegenwart. Festschrift für Cord Meckseper zum 65. Geburtstag. Petersberg: Imhof, pp. 77–84.

Binding, Günther (2003): "Architekturzeichnung." In: Lexikon des Mittelalters, Bd. 1, München: dtv, pp. 906 –907.

Binding, Günther (2004): Meister der Baukunst. Geschichte des Architekten- und Ingenieurberufs. Darmstadt: Wissenschaftliche Buchgesellschaft.

Binding, Günther (2006): Was ist Gotik? Eine Analyse der gotischen Kirchen in Frankreich, England und Deutschland 1140–1350. Darmstadt: Wissenschaftliche Buchgesellschaft.

Binding, Günther (2010a): "Zahl und Geometrie als Gestaltungsgrundlagen: *ordo* und *pulchritudo*." In: Insitu – Zeitschrift für Architekturgeschichte 2 (2010), No. 2, pp. 149–164.

Binding, Günther (2010b): "*Forma, figura* und *schema* – ein Hinweis auf geometrisch bestimmte Baupläne im frühen und hohen Mittelalter?" In: Mittellateinisches Jahrbuch 45 (2010), No. 3, pp. 459–468.

Binding, Günther (2012): Der mittelalterliche Baubetrieb in zeitgenössischen Abbildungen. Darmstadt: Wissenschaftliche Buchgesellschaft.

Binding, Günther (2014): "Bauwissen im Früh- und Hochmittelalter." In: Renn, Jürgen / Wilhelm Osthues / Hermann Schlimme (Eds.): Wissensgeschichte der Architektur. Band III: Vom Mittelalter bis zur Frühen Neuzeit. Berlin: Neopubli, Edition open-access, pp. 9–94. URL: http://edition-open-access.de/studies/5/3/index.html (02/23/2018).

Binding, Günther (2015): Bauvermessung und Proportion im frühen und hohen Mittelalter. (Monographien zur Geschichte des Mittelalters, Bd. 61. Hrsg. von Alfred Haverkamp.) Stuttgart: Anton Hiersemann Verlag.

Binding, Günther (2016): "Baubezogene Begriffe bei Vitruv sowie in spätantiken und mittelalterlichen Quellen. Ein Beitrag zur Problematik fachgerechter Übersetzung." In: Mittellateinisches Jahrbuch 51 (2016), No. 2, pp. 195–220.

Binding, Günther / Linscheid-Burdich, Susanne (2002): Planen und Bauen im frühen und hohen Mittelalter nach den Schriftquellen bis 1250. Darmstadt: Wissenschaftliche Buchgesellschaft.

Bloom, Jonathan M. (1993): "On the transmission of designs in early islamic architecture." In: Muqarnas 10 (1993), pp. 21–28, URL: https://archnet.org/publications/4131 (02/16/2018).

Bloom, Jonathan M. (2001): Paper before Print. The History and Impact of Paper in the Islamic World. New Haven / London: Yale University Press.

Böker, Johann Josef / Brehm, Anne-Christine et al. (Eds.) (2013): Architektur der Gotik. Rheinlande. Ein Bestandskatalog der mittelalterlichen Architekturzeichnungen. Salzburg: Verlag Muery Salzmann.

Booz, Paul (1956): Der Baumeister der Gotik. München / Berlin: Deutscher Kunstverlag.

Bork, Robert (2016): The Geometry of Creation. Architectural Drawing and the Dynamics of Gothic Design. London: Routledge.

Branner, Robert (1958): "Drawings from a 13th-Century Architect's Shop: The Reims Palimpsest." In: Journal of the Society of Architectural Historians 17 (1958), No. 4, pp. 9–21.

Branner, Robert (1963): "Villard de Honnecourt, Reims and the Origin of Gothic Architectural Drawing." In: Gazette des Beaux-Arts 105 (1963), pp. 129–146.

Bridges, Margaret (2005): "Mehr als ein Text. Das ungelesene Buch zwischen Symbol und Fetisch." In: Stolz, Michael / Mettauer, Adrian (Eds.): Buchkultur im Mittelalter. Schrift – Bild – Kommunikation. Berlin / New York: De Gruyter, pp. 103–121.

Brooks, George (2008): "Villard de Honnecourt: Gothic Carpenter." In: Avista Forum Journal 18.1/2, pp. 8–23.

Brunner-Traut, Emma (1990): Frühformen des Erkennens am Beispiel Altägyptens. Darmstadt: Wissenschaftliche Buchgesellschaft.

Bucher, François (1968): "Design in Gothic Architecture. A Preliminary Assessment." Journal of the Society of Architectural Historians Vol. 27, No. 1 (1968), pp. 49–71. URL: http://jsah.ucpress.edu/content/ncpjsah/27/1/49.full.pdf (04/13/2018).

Buringh, Eltjo / van Zanden, Jan Luiten (2009): "Charting the 'Rise of the West': Manuscripts and Printed Books in Europe. A Long-Term Perspective from the Sixth through Eighteenth Centuries." In: The Journal of Economic History, June 2009, pp. 1–54. URL: https://www.researchgate.net/publication/46544350 (12/29/2018).

Büker, Dieter (2020): In neuem Licht – Der Klosterplan von St. Gallen. Aspekte seiner Beschaffenheit und Erschaffung mit einem Beitrag von Alfons Zettler. Berlin: Peter Lang.

Butschek, Felix (2006): Industrialisierung. Ursachen, Verlauf, Konsequenzen. Wien / Köln / Weimar: Böhlau.

Camerota, Filippo (2004): "Renaissance Descriptive Geometry: The Codification of Drawing Methods." In: Lefèvre, Wolfgang (Ed.): Picturing Machines 1400–1700. Cambridge / London: The MIT Press, pp. 175–208.

Coenen, Ulrich (2009): "Architekturtheorie und Entwurfslehre im Mittelalter." In: Johannes, Ralph (Ed.): Entwerfen. Architektenausbildung in Europa von Vitruv bis Mitte des 20. Jahrhunderts. Geschichte – Theorie – Praxis. Hamburg: Junius, pp. 196–214.

Conrad, Dietrich (1998): Kirchenbau im Mittelalter. Bauplanung und Bauausführung. Berlin: Edition Leipzig, 3. Auflage.

De Padova, Thomas (2021): Alles wird Zahl. Wie sich die Mathematik in der Renaissance neu erfand. München: Hanser.

Eisenlohr, Erika (1997): "Die Kunst, Pergament zu machen." In: Lindgren, Uta (Ed.): Europäische Technik im Mittelalter. 800 bis 1400. Tradition und Innovation. Ein Handbuch. Berlin: Gebr. Mann Verlag, 2. Auflage, pp. 429–434.

Engelsing, Rolf (1973): Analphabetentum und Lektüre. Zur Sozialgeschichte des Lesens in Deutschland zwischen feudaler und industrieller Gesellschaft. Stuttgart: J. B. Metzlersche Verlagsbuchhandlung.

Fondation de l'Oeuvre Notre-Dame (Eds.) (without year): Dessins. Cathédrale de Strasbourg. Musée de l'Oeuvre Notre-Dame, Strasbourg.

Folkerts, Menso (2002): "Geometrie – gelehrte Kreise von Sizilien bis Oxford." In: Spektrum der Wissenschaft Spezial 2 (2002): Forschung und Technik im Mittelalter, pp. 26–31.

Friedman, John Block (1974): "The Architect's Compass in Creation Miniatures of the Later Middle Ages." In: Traditio. Studies in Ancient and Medieval History, Thought, and Religion Vol. XXX (1974), pp. 419–429.

Frugoni, Chiara (2004): Das Mittelalter auf der Nase. Brillen, Bücher, Bankgeschäfte und andere Erfindungen des Mittelalters. München: C. H. Beck. [Ital. Original: Medioevo sul naso. Occhiali, bottoni e altre invenzioni medievali. Rom. Engl. Translation: Books, Banks, Buttons and other Inventions from the Middle Ages. 2003. Fr. Translation: Le Moyen Âge sur le bout du nez. Lunettes, boutons et autres inventions médiévales. 2011.]

Gasparinetti, Andrea F. (2006): "Carte, cartiere e cartai fabrianesi." / "The Fabrianese Paper, Papermills and Papermakers." In: Castagnari, Giancarlo (Ed.): Carta – cartiere – cartai. La thematica storica di Andrea Gasparinetti. Paper – Papermills – Papermakers. The Historical Theme of Andrea Gasparinetti. Fabriano: Pia Università dei Cartai, pp. 62–68 and pp. 227–259.

Gimpel, Jean (1980): Die industrielle Revolution des Mittelalters. Zürich / München: Artemis. [Fr. Original: La révolution industrielle du Moyen Age. Paris 1975. Engl. translation: Medieval Machine. The Industrial Revolution of the Middle Ages. 1977.]

Gimpel, Jean (1996): Die Kathedralenbauer. Mit einem Vorwort von Ken Follett. Aus dem Französischen von Katharina Kramer. Holm: Deukalion. [Fr. Original: Les bâtisseurs de cathédrales. Seuil 1980. Engl. Translation: The Cathedral Builders. 1992]

Göttert, Karl-Heinz (2011): Deutsch. Biografie einer Sprache. Berlin: Ullstein, 4. Auflage.

Hecht, Konrad (1979): Maß und Zahl in der gotischen Baukunst. Hildesheim / New York: Georg Olms Verlag.

Ifrah, Georges (1991): Universalgeschichte der Zahlen. Frankfurt a. M. / New York: Campus, 2. Auflage. [Fr. Original: Histoire universelle des Chiffres. Paris 1981. Engl. Translation: The Universal History of Numbers. From Prehistory to the Invention of the Computer. 2000.]

Illich, Ivan / Sanders, Barry (1988): Das Denken lernt schreiben. Lesekultur und Identität. Hamburg: Hoffmann und Campe. [Engl. Original: A.B.C. Alphabetization of the Popular Mind. 1988. Fr. Translation: ABC. L'alphabetization de l'esprit populaire. 1990.]

Illich, Ivan (1991): Im Weinberg des Textes. Als das Schriftbild der Moderne entstand. Ein Kommentar zu Hugos 'Didascalicon'. Aus dem Englischen von Yla Eriksson-Kuchenbuch. Frankfurt: Luchterhand. [Fr. Original: L'Ere du livre. Paris 1990. Engl. Translation: In the Vineyard of the Text. A Commentary to Hugh's Didascalicon. 2022.]

Johannes, Ralph (Ed.) (2009): Entwerfen. Architektenausbildung in Europa von Vitruv bis Mitte des 20. Jahrhunderts. Geschichte – Theorie – Praxis. Hamburg: Junius.

Kadeřávek, František (1992): Geometrie und Kunst in früherer Zeit. Nach dem 1935 in Prag erschienenen Original aus dem Tschechischen übersetzt von Leo Boček und Zbyněk Nádenik. Stuttgart / Leipzig: B. G. Teubner Verlagsgesellschaft.

Kimpel, Dieter / Suckale, Robert (1985): Die gotische Architektur in Frankreich 1130–1270. München: Hirmer Verlag.

Kimpel, Dieter (1989): "Die Soziogenese des Architektenberufs." In: Möbius, Friedrich / Sciurie, Helga (Eds.): Stil und Epoche. Dresden: VEB Verlag der Kunst, pp. 106–143.

Kintzinger, Martin (2007): Wissen wird Macht. Bildung im Mittelalter. Ostfildern: Jan Thorbecke.

Klein, Rudolf (2014): "Unser arabisches Erbe – wie die Null nach Europa kam." Akademie Berlingen. URL: https://www.akademie-berlingen.ch/wp-content/uploads/Arabisches-Erbe.pdf (02/26/2018).

Kletzl, Otto (1939): Plan-Fragmente aus der deutschen Dombauhütte von Prag in Stuttgart und Ulm. (Veröffentlichungen des Archivs der Stadt Stuttgart Heft 3.) Stuttgart: Felix Krais Verlag.

Klein, Bruno (2001): "Der Fassadenplan 5 für das Straßburger Münster und der Beginn des fiktiven Architekturentwurfs." In: Lieb, Stefanie (Ed.): Form und Stil. Festschrift für Günther Binding zum 65. Geburtstag. Darmstadt: Wissenschaftliche Buchgesellschaft, pp. 166-174.

Klug, Sonja Ulrike (2002): "Die Heilige Geometrie der Kathedrale von Chartres." In: Grenzgebiete der Wissenschaft 51 (2002), pp. 3–18.

Klug, Sonja Ulrike (2007): Chartres – der Kathedralführer. Geschichte, Architektur, Schule, Skulpturen, Labyrinth und Glasfenster der französischen Kathedrale. Bad Honnef: Kluges Verlag.

Klug, Sonja Ulrike (2008): Kathedrale des Kosmos. Die heilige Geometrie von Chartres. Bad Honnef: Kluges Verlag, 3rd ed.

Klug, Sonja Ulrike (2021): "Bau- und Konstruktionsplanung im Mittelalter. Wie die Frage nach den 'verschollenen' Werkrissen zu beantworten ist." In: Insitu – Zeitschrift für Architekturgeschichte 13 (2021), No. 2, pp. 193–206.

Klug, Sonja Ulrike (2022a): Zirkel und Zeichenkunst. Wie romanische und gotische Kathedralen entworfen und geplant wurden. Fokus Mittelalter. Bad Honnef: Kluges Verlag.

Klug, Sonja Ulrike (2022b): Chartres kompakt. Die gotische Kathedrale im Überblick. Bad Honnef: Kluges Verlag.

Lefèvre, Wolfgang (Ed.) (2004a): Picturing Machines 1400–1700. Cambridge / London: The MIT Press.

Lefèvre, Wolfgang (2004b): "The Emergence of Combined Orthographic Projections." In: Lefèvre, Wolfgang (Ed.) (2004a), pp. 209–244.

Lepik, Andres (2011): "Erfindung eines Mediums. Architekturmodelle in der frühen Renaissance." In: Zuschnitt 44, Denkraum Holz. URL: https://www.proholz.at/zuschnitt/44/erfindung-eines-mediums (09/03/2023)

Lingohr, Michael (2009): "'Architectus' – Überlegungen zu einem vor- und frühneuzeitlichen Berufsbild." In: Johannes, Ralph (Ed.), pp. 46–65.

Marquart, Markus (2013): „Metallische Schreibgriffel des hohen Mittelalters aus Aschaffenburg und ihre Vergleiche." In: Aschaffenburger Jahrbuch 29 (2013), pp. 9–63.

Mazal, Otto (1994): "Traditionelle Schreibmaterialien und -techniken." In: Günther, Hartmut / Ludwig, Otto et al. (Eds.): Schrift und Schriftlichkeit. Writing and Its Use. Ein interdisziplinäres Handbuch internationaler Forschung. An Interdisciplinary Handbook of International Research. 1. Halbband. Handbücher zur Sprach- und Kommunikationswissenschaft, Bd. 10.1. Berlin / New York: De Gruyter Verlag, pp. 122–130.

Meynen, Gloria (2003): "Routen und Routinen." In: Siegert, Bernhard / Vogl, Joseph (Eds.): Europa: Kultur der Sekretäre. Zürich / Berlin: Diaphanes, pp. 195–219.

Monro, Alexander (2014): Papier. Wie eine chinesische Erfindung die Welt revolutionierte. München: Bertelsmann. [Engl. Translation: The Paper Trail. An Unexpected History of an Revolutionary Invention. 2017.]

Müller, Herbert (2013): Entwurfsgeheimnisse der Kirchenbaumeister der Lübecker Marienkirche. Wismar: Förderverein der Stadtbibliothek Wismar e.V.

Müller, Herbert (2015): Zahlen und Geometrie beim Bauwerksentwurf in alten Zeiten – eine Neubetrachtung. Betrachtungsschwerpunkt: Gotische Backsteinkirchen im südlichen Ostseeraum. Wismar: Förderverein der Stadtbibliothek Wismar e.V.

Müller, Werner (1990): Grundlagen gotischer Bautechnik. Ars sine scientia nihil. München: Deutscher Kunstverlag.

Müller, Werner (2002): Steinmetzgeometrie zwischen Spätgotik und Barock. Eine Bautechnik auf dem Wege vom Handwerk zur Ingenieurwissenschaft. Petersberg: Imhof.

Nagl, Manfred (2019): Gotik und Informatik. Intelligenter Entwurf damals und heute. Wiesbaden: SpringerVieweg.

Neddermeyer, Uwe (1998): Von der Handschrift zum gedruckten Buch: Schriftlichkeit und Leseinteresse im Mittelalter und der frühen Neuzeit. Quantitative und qualitative Aspekte. Band 1: Text. (Buchwissenschaftliche Beiträge aus dem Deutschen Bucharchiv München, Bd. 61.) Köln, Univ., Habil.-Schr. 1996. Wiesbaden: Harrassowitz.

Needham, Joseph / Tsuen-Hsuin, Tsien (1985): Science and Civilisation in China. Vol. 5: Chemistry and Chemical Technology. Part I: Paper and Printing. Cambridge: Cambridge University Press.

Ong, Walter J. (2016): Oralität und Literalität. Die Technologisierung des Wortes. Wiesbaden: Springer, 2. Auflage. [Engl. Original: Orality and Literacy. The Technologizing of the Word. London, 1982/2002. Fr. Translation: Oralité et Écriture. La technologie de la parole. 2014.]

Osthues, Wilhelm (2014): "Bauwissen im Antiken Griechenland." In: Renn, Jürgen / Osthues, Wilhelm / Schlimme, Hermann (Eds.): Wissensgeschichte der Architektur. Band II: Vom Alten Ägypten bis zum Antiken Rom. Berlin: Neopubli, Edition open-access, pp. 127–261. URL: http://edition-open-access.de/studies/5/3/index.html (25.02.2018).

Ott, Norbert H. (2000): "Texte und Bilder. Beziehungen zwischen den Medien Kunst und Literatur in Mittelalter und früher Neuzeit." In: Wenzel, Horst / Seipel, Wilfried / Wunberg, Gotthart (Eds.): Die Verschriftlichung der Welt. Bild, Text und Zahl in der Kultur des Mittelalters und der Frühen Neuzeit. Schriften des Kunsthistorischen Museums, Bd. 5. Wien: Kunsthistorisches Museum, pp. 105–143.

Pause, Peter (1973): Gotische Architekturzeichnungen in Deutschland. Diss. Phil. Bonn.

Peiffer, Jeanne (2004): "Projections embodied in technical drawings: Dürer and his Followers." In: Lefèvre, Wolfgang (Ed.) (2004a), pp. 245–275.

Pfeifer, Wolfgang (2012): Etymologisches Wörterbuch des Deutschen. Koblenz: Edition Kramer.

Philipp, Klaus Jan (2002): "Himmelwärts – Bauen zum Lobe Gottes." In: Spektrum der Wissenschaft Spezial 2 (2002): Forschung und Technik im Mittelalter, pp. 80–83.

Popplow, Marcus (2006): "Unsichere Karrieren: Ingenieure in Mittelalter und Früher Neuzeit 500 – 1750." In: Kaiser, Walter / König, Wolfgang (Eds.): Geschichte des Ingenieurs. Ein Beruf in sechs Jahrtausenden. München: Hanser, pp. 71–125.

Popplow, Marcus (2010): Technik im Mittelalter. München: C. H. Beck.

Reidinger, Erwin (2014): 1027 – Gründung des Speyrer Doms. Sonne – Orientierung – Achsknick – Gründungsdatum – Erzengel Michael. Speyer: Pilgerverlag.

Rüffer, Jens (2014): Werkprozess – Wahrnehmung – Interpretation: Studien zur mittelalterlichen Gestaltungspraxis und zur Methodik und Erschließung am Beispiel baugebundener Struktur. Berlin: Lukas Verlag.

Ruggieri, Nicola (2017): "Macchine, Strumenti, Utensìli e attrezzi di cantiere a Pompei nel I secolo D.C." in: Bollettino ingegneri 9-10 (2017), pp. 16–28. URL: https://www.researchgate.net/publication/322888011 (12.07.2019).

Sandermann, Wilhelm (1988): Papier. Eine spannende Kulturgeschichte. Berlin: Springer Verlag.

Santifaller, Leo (1953): Beiträge zur Geschichte der Beschreibstoffe im Mittelalter. Mit besonderer Berücksichtigung der päpstlichen Kanzlei. 1. Teil: Untersuchungen. Mitteilungen des Instituts für Österreichische Geschichtsforschung, Ergänzungsband XVI, Heft 1, Graz: Böhlau.

Schäfke, Werner (1979): Frankreichs gotische Kathedralen. Eine Reise zu den Höhepunkten mittelalterlicher Architektur in Frankreich. Köln: DuMont.

Schillinger, Klaus (Ed.) (1990): Zeicheninstrumente. Katalog. Staatlicher Mathematisch-Physikalischer Salon Dresden, Zwinger. Dresden. URL: https://books.ub.uni-heidelberg.de/arthistoricum/reader/download/15/15-16-117-1-10-20140911.pdf (03/03/2020).

Schlink, Wilhelm (1999): "War Villard de Honnecourt Analphabet?" In: Joubert, Fabienne / Sandron, Dany (1999): Pierre, lumière, couleur: Études d'histoire et de l'art du Moyen Age. Paris: Presse de l'Université des Paris-Sorbonne. (Sonderdrucke der Albert-Ludwigs-Universität Freiburg). URL: https://freidok.uni-freiburg.de/dnb/download/449 (01/02/2018).

Schmidt, Frieder (2002): "Medientechnik – vom Pergament zum Papier." In: Spektrum der Wissenschaft Spezial 2 (2002): Forschung und Technik im Mittelalter, pp. 86–89.

Schneegans, Friedrich Ed. (1901): "Ueber die Sprache des Skizzenbuches von Vilard de Honnecourt." In: Zeitschrift für Romanische Philologie 25 (1901), pp. 45–70.

Schneider, Ivo (1970): Der Proportionalzirkel. Ein universelles Analogrecheninstrument der Vergangenheit. Deutsches Museum, Abhandlungen und Berichte, 38. Jahrgang, Heft 2. München / Düsseldorf: Oldenbourg Verlag / VDI-Verlag.

Schneider, Karin (2014): Paläographie und Handschriftenkunde für Germanisten. Eine Einführung. Berlin / New York: De Gruyter, 3. Auflage.

Schock-Werner, Barbara (2009): "Die Ausbildung der Architekten im Mittelalter." In: Johannes, Ralph (Ed.), pp. 186–195.

Schöller, Wolfgang (1989): "Ritzzeichnungen. Ein Beitrag zur Geschichte der Architekturzeichnung im Mittelalter." In: Architectura: Zeitschrift für Geschichte der Baukunst 19 (1989), pp. 36–61.

Schreiber, Peter (2002): "Algorithmen – Programme für den Handbetrieb." In: Spektrum der Wissenschaft Spezial 2 (2002): Forschung und Technik im Mittelalter, pp. 16–19.

Schuler, Stefan (1999): "Vitruvs 'De architectura' und die Baukunst in der Enzyklopädie des Vinzenz von Beauvais: Kompilation und Innovation." In: Keller, Hagen / Meier, Christel / Scharff, Thomas (Eds.): Schriftlichkeit und Lebenspraxis im Mittelalter. Erfassen, Bewahren, Verändern. Akten des Internationalen Kolloquiums 8. bis 10. Juni 1995. Münstersche Mittelalter-Schriften 96. München: Fink Verlag, pp. 243–266. URL: www.uni-muenster.de/Fruehmittelalter/Publikationen/mms/idex.html (04/16/2018).

Scriba, Christoph C. / Schreiber, Peter (2000): 5000 Jahre Geometrie. Geschichte, Kulturen, Menschen. Berlin / Heidelberg: Springer.

Shelby, Lon R. (1965): "Medieval Masons' Tools. II. Compass and Square." In: Technology and Culture, Vol. 6, No. 2 (1965), pp. 236–248. URL: http://www.designspeculum.com/Historyweb/shelby%20medieval%20masons%20tools%20II.pdf (07/21/2019).

Shelby, Lon R. (1971): "Medieval Masons' Templates." In: The Journal of the Society of Architectural Historians, Vol. 30, No. 2 (1971), pp. 140–154. URL: www.designspeculum.com/Historyweb/shelby%20templates.pdf (02/10/2018).

Shelby, Lon R. (1972): "The Geometrical Knowledge of Medieval Master Masons." In: Speculum, Vol. 47, No. 3 (1972), pp. 395–421. URL: www.designspeculum.com/Historyweb/shelby%20-%20geometry.pdf (02/10/2018).

Skrzypcak, Henryk A. (1956): Stadt und Schriftlichkeit im deutschen Mittelalter. Diss. phil. Berlin.

Steinmann, Marc (2003): Die Westfassade des Kölner Doms. Der mittelalterliche Fassadenplan F. Forschungen zum Kölner Dom I. (Ed. by Barbara Schock-Werner and Rolf Lauer.) Köln: Verlag Kölner Dom.

Steinmann, Marc (2014): "Die mittelalterlichen Planzeichnungen des Kölner Domes. Zum Versuch einer Spätdatierung im Corpuswerk der mittelalterlichen Architekturzeichnungen." In: Kölner Domblatt. Jahrbuch des Zentral-Dombau-Vereins. Im Auftrage des Vorstandes hrsg. von der Dombauhütte Köln. Köln: Verlag Kölner Dom, pp. 294–303.

Stiegemann, Christoph (2018): "Gotik prägt Europa. Paderborn feiert den Dom und die Baukultur des 13. Jahrhunderts in einer großen Ausstellung." In: Rotary Magazin September 2018, pp. 67–69.

Universität Bamberg / AB (2020): "Notre Dame in Paris: 3D-Daten für den Wiederaufbau." URL: https://www.archaeologie-online.de/nachrichten/notre-dame-in-paris-3d-daten-fuer-den-wiederaufbau-4524/ (02/17/2020).

Valls i Subira, Oriol (1978): The History of Paper in Spain. X – XIV Centuries. Madrid.

Villard de Honnecourt (ca. 1235): Album de dessins et croquis. URL: http://gallica.bnf.fr/ark:/12148/btv1b105094122/f75.image, and URL: https://archive.org/details/albumdevillarddeoovill/mode/2up (04/30/2020).

Vitruv, [Pollio, Marcus] (1964): De Architectura libri decem. Zehn Bücher über Architektur. Übersetzt und mit Anmerkungen versehen von Dr. Curt Fensterbusch. Darmstadt: Wissenschaftliche Buchgesellschaft.

Völkle, Peter (2013): "Die Zeichentechnik der Gotik: Materialien, Werkzeuge und Zeichenvorgang." In: Böker, Johann Josef / Brehm, Anne-Christine et al. (Eds.), pp. 14–23.

Vollrath, Hans-Joachim / Weigand, Hans-Georg / Weth, Thomas (2000): "Spezialisierung und Generalisierung in der Entwicklung der Zirkel." In: Liedtke, M. (Ed.): Relikte – der Mensch und seine Kultur. Matreier Gespräche. Graz: Austria Medien Service, pp. 123–158. URL: http://www.history.didaktik.mathematik.uni-wuerzburg.de/vollrath/papers/zirkel.pdf (06/20/2019).

Wendehorst, Alfred (1986): "Wer konnte im Mittelalter lesen und schreiben?" In: Fried, Johannes (Ed.): Schulen und Studium im sozialen Wandel des hohen und späten Mittelalters. Vorträge und Forschungen, Bd. XXX, hg. vom Konstanzer Arbeitskreis für mittelalterliche Geschichte. Stuttgart: Jan Thorbecke, pp. 9–32. URL: https://journals.ub.uni-heidelberg.de/index.php/vuf/article/viewFile/15806/9674 (02/20/2018).

Wenzel, Horst (1995): Hören und Sehen. Schrift und Bild. Kultur und Gedächtnis im Mittelalter. München: C. H. Beck.

Wertheim, Margaret (2000): Die Himmelstür zum Cyberspace. Von Dante zum Internet. Zürich: Ammann Verlag. [Engl. Original: Pearly Gates of Cyberspace – A History of Space from Dante to the Internet. New York, 1999.]

6.4 Picture Credits

Cover: Proportional compass by Heinrich Stolle, Prague 1625-1700, Gründungssammlung des Deutschen Museums, edited by Julia Bloemer and Benjamin Mitwald, Vs. 2016/08/24, https://digital.deutsches-museum.de/projekte/gruendungssammlung/ (CC BY-SA); https://commons.wikimedia.org/wiki/File:Villard_de_Honnecourt_-_Sketchbook_-_30.jpg (public domain); cf. fig. 10; cf. fig. 11

Fig. 1 and p. 7: https://de.wikipedia.org/wiki/St._Galler_Klosterplan#/media/Datei:Codex_Sangallensis_1092_recto.jpg (public domain)

Fig. 2, 13, 17, 18, 22, 29, 30, 38: Sonja Ulrike Klug

Fig. 3: https://de.wikipedia.org/wiki/Pergament#/media/Datei:Permennter-1568.png (public domain)

Fig. 4: B. Simpson Cairocamels https://de.wikipedia.org/wiki/Datei:Blank_papyrus_paper.jpg (public domain) - Membeth https://de.wikipedia.org/wiki/Datei:Pergament.1.jpg (CC0 1.0)

Fig. 5: SLUB Dresden / Digitale Sammlungen /Mechan. 35, misc. 1

Fig. 6: Accademia delle Scienze Turin https://commons.wikimedia.org/wiki/Category:Villard_de_Honnecourt?uselang=de#/media/File:Disegni_e_didascalie,_XIII_secolo_-_Archivio_Accademia_delle_Scienze_Torino,_Millon_48_14_146.jpg (public domain)

Fig. 7: Herzog August Bibliothek Wolfenbüttel, http://diglib.hab.de/mss/114-1-extrav/start.htm?image=0009 (Cod. Guelf. 114.1 Extrav.) (public domain, CC BY-SA 4.0)

Fig. 8 and p. 17: https://commons.wikimedia.org/wiki/File:Notker_Balbulus_2.jpg (public domain)

Fig. 9: https://commons.wikimedia.org/wiki/Category:Villard_de_Honne-court?uselang=de#/media/File:Villard_de_Honnecourt.jpg (public domain)

Fig. 10 and p. 213: https://commons.wikimedia.org/wiki/Category:Tower_of_Babel_in_medieval_miniature?uselang=de#/media/File:Maciejowski_Tower_of_Babel.jpg (public domain)

Fig. 11: https://en.wikipedia.org/wiki/Strasbourg_Cathedral#/media/File:Dessin_A'.jpg (public domain)

Fig. 12: Palauenco5 https://commons.wikimedia.org/wiki/Category:Hugues_Libergier#/media/File:Reims_Cathedral_Hugues_Libergier.jpg (CC BY-SA 4.0)

Fig. 14: https://de.wikipedia.org/wiki/Datei:WP_K%C3%B6lner_Dom_Riss_F.jpg (public domain)

Fig. 15: https://en.wikipedia.org/wiki/Strasbourg_Cathedral#/media/File:Jean_Gerlach_de_Steinbach,_Dessin_5.jpg (public domain)

Fig. 16: Redrawn and colored by Sonja Ulrike Klug, based on British Library, Add. Ms. 15692 fol. 29v

Fig. 19 and p. 81 Dnalor_01 https://de.wikipedia.org/wiki/Hortus_Deliciarum#/media/Datei:Hortus_Deliciarum,_Die_Philosophie_mit_den_sieben_freien_K%C3%BCnsten.JPG (CC BY-SA 3.0)

Fig. 20: Snrec https://en.wikipedia.org/wiki/Codex_Vigilanus#/media/File:Codex_Vigilanus_Primeros_Numeros_Arabigos.jpg (public domain), creative design as parchment by Sonja Ulrike Klug

Fig. 21: Gregor Reisch https://commons.wikimedia.org/wiki/Category:Gregor_Reisch_-_Margarita_Philosophica_-_Typus_Arithmeticae?uselang=de#/media/File:Gregor_Reisch_-_Margarita_Philosophica_-_Arithmetica.jpg (public domain)

Fig. 23: Frontispiece of an Adelard of Bath Latin translation of Euclid's Elements, British Library Manuscript 275, c. 14th centure, attributed to Meliacin Master https://en.wikipedia.org/wiki/Adelard_of_Bath#/media/File:Woman_teaching_geometry.jpg (public domain)

Fig. 24: According to Mathes Roriczer, Geometria Deutsch 1487/88 (Creative color scheme by Sonja Ulrike Klug)

Fig. 25: https://www.researchgate.net/figure/Diverse-tipologie-di-compassi-conservati-nel-Museo-Archeologico-Nazionale-di-Napoli-in_fig4_322888011, unknown photographer, early 20th century

Fig. 26: Württembergische Landesbibliothek, Etymologiae 1-16, Cod.Poet.et.phil.fol.33, f. 28, https://digital.wlb-stuttgart.de/sammlungen/sammlungsliste/werksansicht?id=6&tx_dlf%5Border%5D=title&tx_dlf%5Bid%5D=18031&tx_dlf%5Bpage%5D=60, Creative redesign and color scheme by Sonja Ulrike Klug

Fig. 27, 40: Universitätsbibliothek Heidelberg, Coloring and colored border by Sonja Ulrike Klug

Fig. 28: Based on Dublin Trinity College, TCD, Ms. 177, Fol. 59v, https://commons.wikimedia.org/wiki/Category:Dublin,_Trinity_College,_MS_E._I._40,_Life_of_St._Alban?uselang=de#/media/File:Brouette_Matthew_Paris.jpg (CC BY-SA 3.0)

Fig. 31: https://de.wikipedia.org/wiki/Datei:Buergi_zirkelgross.jpg (public domain)

Fig. 32: Kurt Schwitters https://de.m.wikipedia.org/wiki/Datei:GoldenerZirkel.jpg (CC)

Fig. 33: Daderot https://en.m.wikipedia.org/wiki/File:Sector_with_dividers,_probably_Dresden,_c._1630_-_Mathematisch-Physikalischer_Salon,_Dresden_-_DSC08048.JPG (public domain)

Fig. 34: Based on Codex Vindobonensis 2554 (ÖNB), https://commons.wikimedia.org/wiki/File:God-Architect.jpg (public domain)

Fig. 35: https://de.wikipedia.org/wiki/Moritz_Ensinger#/media/Datei:Moritz_Ensinger.jpg (public domain)

Fig. 36: Redesigned by Sonja Ulrike Klug, based on the original from the Museo di Torcello, Venice

Fig. 37: Redesigned by Sonja Ulrike Klug, based on the original from the Museum August Kestner, Hanover

Fig. 39 and p. 137: Albrecht Dürer, https://collections.nlm.nih.gov/catalog/nlm:nlmuid-2233015R-bk (public domain)

Fig. 41 and p. 207: https://de.wikipedia.org/wiki/Datei:Baumeister_-_Holzschnitt_von_Jost_Amman_-_1536.svg (public domain)

Icons, p. 2, 13ff.: https://de.freepik.com

6.5 Acknowledgement

I would like to express my gratitude to **Prof. Dr.-Ing. Dr. phil. Günther Binding** for his meticulous review, which enabled me to correct some errors and incorporate key insights prior to publication. Given the prevalence of inaccuracies regarding medieval construction plans in architectural historical research, which have woven themselves into the literature like "false threads" and are difficult to remove, his input was invaluable. While I did diverge from Binding's suggestions on a few matters due to my own perspective, I greatly appreciate his assistance.

6.6 About the author

Dr. phil. Sonja Ulrike Klug obtained her doctorate in Linguistics and currently works as a freelance writer. Her academic interest lies in medieval cathedrals and their construction, which she has been researching for over two decades. In addition to books on other topics, she published six books and several professional articles on the subject of cathedrals.

Dr. Klug's German work "Kathedrale des Kosmos" has been translated into Portuguese and Italian. It explores the "sacred geometry" of Chartres in narrative form. "Chartres kompakt" provides an objective overview of Chartres Cathedral.

The German edition of this book was published in 2020 under the title "Zauberer des Zirkels".

Dr. Klug offers lectures on the subjects covered in her publications upon request.

Contact: info@buchbetreuung-klug.com

Made in United States
Cleveland, OH
23 December 2024

12581153R00133